Praise for
THIS ISN'T HAPPENING

"In this brilliant book, Steven Hyden goes deep into why *Kid A* matters—it's the fascinating saga of how the music turned into the symbol of a new cultural era."　　　**—Rolling Stone**

"[Hyden is] one of America's foremost rock critics."
　　　　　　　　　　　　　　　　　—Wall Street Journal

"*This Isn't Happening* is a foundational text for understanding a difficult, prophetic album, and an addictive read for any fan of Radiohead."　　　　　　　　　　　**—BuzzFeed**

"With the conversational irreverence of the guy sitting down at the bar, Hyden draws connections to hybrid rock acts like Linkin Park, surreal and misanthropic blockbusters like *Fight Club* and *Vanilla Sky*, the internet's transformation from a utopian dream into a dystopian nightmare, and the tragedy on 9/11. For good measure (and fan service), he bookends *This Isn't Happening*'s cultural insights with key Radiohead-related events occurring before and after the album."　　　　　　　**—Pitchfork**

"Hyden provides a thorough primer on the *sound* of *Kid A*. . . . But Hyden truly excels at illuminating the *context* of *Kid A*, from the prerelease expectations to the oft-rapturous reviews to the music's ultimate legacy."

—*The Ringer*

"One of 2020's finest and most enthralling reads . . . there are few folks writing about music with the intelligence, personality, and pop-culture savvy of Steven Hyden."

—*The Film Stage*

"Eminently readable . . . [and] enthralling."

—*Bad Feeling Magazine*

"Outstanding . . . an absolute masterclass in not only sharing [Steven Hyden's] love for an album he obviously adores, and shows a deep respect for, but also a delve into their discography and the impact on his life."

—*Critical Popcorn*

"[Hyden] writes like the best kind of music fan: informed and inviting. . . . A knowledgeable, earnest, always persuasive testament to a cultural touchstone."

—*Kirkus Reviews*

"*This Isn't Happening* is not only an excellent way to revisit *Kid A* but also a springboard for thinking about the shifting fortunes of rock music, the Internet, and the uneasy century we've been living in for the last twenty years."

—**Ezra Koenig of Vampire Weekend**

"If there was ever an album that deserves a book-length exegesis, it's *Kid A*, and there's no one better than Steven Hyden to unpack its mythologies and prophecies, and the extraordinary way it appeared to set the stage for the century that followed. *This Isn't Happening* is a smart, riveting, and dynamic history of a watershed moment for both music and the world."

—Amanda Petrusich, author of *Do Not Sell at Any Price: The Wild, Obsessive Hunt for the World's Rarest 78rpm Records*

"Even if you've immersed yourself in *Kid A* thousands of times, Steven Hyden's passionately argued and kaleidoscopic *This Isn't Happening* will make you rethink and reimagine Radiohead's most audacious album and its place in cultural history—and history itself."

—David Browne, author of *Dream Brother: The Lives and Music of Jeff and Tim Buckley* and *Crosby, Stills, Nash and Young: The Wild, Definitive Saga of Rock's Greatest Supergroup*

"Radiohead, music, and culture all stood at a crossroads in the year 2000. With insight and grace, Steven Hyden explores the ways in which the *Kid A* album pointed toward a future that no one could have fully imagined—and captured a moment that, two decades later, we're still trying to comprehend."

—Alan Light, author of *The Holy or the Broken: Leonard Cohen, Jeff Buckley, and the Unlikely Ascent of "Hallelujah"* and host of *Debatable* on SiriusXM

"*This Isn't Happening* is beyond a mere analysis of *Kid* A. It is a vast and contextual examination of the world, both inside and outside of Radiohead, leading up to and flowing away from the creation of *Kid* A and its impact on both the band and culture as a whole. Connecting the record to film, politics, current events, and the cultural morass that comprised the final moments of the '90s, Steven Hyden gleefully and with meticulous absurdity dissects, deconstructs, and decodes the first great artistic enigma of the new millennium."

—**Alex Ross Perry, writer/director of *Her Smell,***
Listen Up Philip,* and *The Color Wheel

THIS ISN'T HAPPENING

HAPPENING

RADIOHEAD'S *KID A*

AND THE BEGINNING OF THE 21ST CENTURY

STEVEN HYDEN

hachette
BOOKS

New York

Hachette Books
Hachette Book Group
1290 Avenue of the Americas
New York, NY 10104
HachetteBooks.com
Twitter.com/HachetteBooks
Instagram.com/HachetteBooks

First Trade Paperback Edition: June 2021

Published by Hachette Books, an imprint of Perseus Books, LLC,
a subsidiary of Hachette Book Group, Inc. The Hachette Books
name and logo is a trademark of the Hachette Book Group.

The Hachette Speakers Bureau provides a wide range of authors for speaking events.

To find out more, go to www.hachettespeakersbureau.com or call (866) 376-6591.

The publisher is not responsible for websites (or their content)
that are not owned by the publisher.

Print book interior design by Amy Quinn.

Library of Congress Cataloging-in-Publication Data
Names: Hyden, Steven, 1977– author.
Title: This isn't happening: Radiohead's "Kid A" and the
beginning of the 21st century / Steven Hyden.
Description: First edition. | New York: Hachette Books, 2020. | Includes index.
Identifiers: LCCN 2020011123 | ISBN 9780306845680 (hardcover) |
ISBN 9780306845697 (ebook)
Subjects: LCSH: Radiohead (Musical group). Kid A.
Classification: LCC ML421.R25 H94 2020 | DDC 782.42166092/2 [B]—dc23
LC record available at https://lccn.loc.gov/2020011123

ISBNs: 978-0-306-84568-0 (hardcover), 978-0-306-84567-3 (paperback),
978-0-306-84569-7 (ebook)

Printed in the United States of America

LSC-C

Printing 1, 2021

Also by Steven Hyden

Hard to Handle: The Life and Death of the Black Crowes—
  A Memoir (cowritten with Steve Gorman)
Twilight of the Gods: A Journey to the End of Classic Rock
Your Favorite Band Is Killing Me: What Pop Music Rivalries
  Reveal About the Meaning of Life

Dedicated to the person responsible for putting the video for "Creep" in the MTV Buzz Bin. Without you, none of this would have happened.

CONTENTS

. . . Yet there is no avoiding time, the sea of time, the sea of memory and forgetfulness, the years of promise, gone and unrecoverable, of the land almost allowed to claim its better destiny, only to have the claim jumped by evildoers known all too well, and taken instead and held hostage to the future we must live in now forever.

—Thomas Pynchon

We had access to too much money, too much equipment, and little by little, we went insane.

—Francis Ford Coppola

It annoys me how pretty my voice is.

—Thom Yorke

APOCALYPSE NOW

Future dystopias look that way only from a distance. When you're actually living inside of one, it feels more like . . . a late-night talk show.

In the year 2019—the setting, coincidentally, for *Blade Runner*, the 1982 Ridley Scott film that most influenced how a generation of kids, burnouts, sci-fi freaks, and English rock musicians envisioned the future—the talk show in question is *The Late Show with Stephen Colbert*. And tonight's guest is the tiny, wizened singer for the most respected rock band in the world.

With his long, sandy brown hair and mostly gray beard set against delicate, almost feminine features, he comes bracingly close to resembling a younger, more agitated Willie Nelson. But when he strides out from stage left to the half-enthusiastic applause of an audience partly stocked with Radiohead fans, Thom

Yorke doesn't exactly strike one as having a stoned, Zen-like presence. He's fairly relaxed for *him*, casually dressed in a black jacket, black pants, and white sneakers with no socks. But otherwise his vibe is reminiscent of a lyric from the song "Talk Show Host," which he wrote nearly twenty-five years prior: "I want to be someone else or I'll explode."

But Thom doesn't explode. Instead, he shakes Stephen Colbert's hand, takes a seat, and attempts to approximate the affable demeanor of a normal late-night talk-show guest. But he can't quite pull it off. His banter game is inadequate. He looks down a lot. Picks lint off of his pants. Falls easily into awkward pauses.

When Colbert asks Thom—at the request of his sons, who are apparently huge Radiohead fans—for his favorite R.E.M. song, Yorke mumbles so low that Colbert asks him to repeat his answer.

"'So. Central Rain,'" Thom says again.

Colbert nods and smiles. Then he pivots hard to the first question of the interview.

"For decades you've been writing music that is uneasy and anxious with regards to society, our government, technology, the general direction of the world," Colbert says, carefully setting up his punch line.

"How does it feel to be right?"

The audience bursts into applause. Thom chuckles, but it's one of those chuckles where you laugh because it's true, not because it's funny. It is decidedly *not* funny, in fact, but what can you do *but* laugh?

If a time traveler from the early aughts had somehow ended up in the studio audience that night, she might have noted the oddness of Thom Yorke's walk-on music: A lounge-jazz, sorta-peppy rendition of one of Radiohead's most pulverizing and—here's a word forever linked to Radiohead—*bleakest* tunes, "The National Anthem."

There are no vocals, so the audience is spared the Thom Yorke lyric that truly seemed prescient nearly two decades later, during a time when the apocalypse has been reduced to fodder for tweets, stand-up comedy, and campaign commercials: "Everyone is so near / Everyone has got the fear / It's holding on / It's holding on."

When you live inside of a future dystopia, you can't really stop and comment on the omnipresent bleakness. When "bleak" is right *there*, it is no longer bleak. The fear is so near you can't even see it. It is just . . . normal.

Cue the APPLAUSE sign.

While Stephen Colbert didn't mention it by name, the Radiohead album that most epitomizes the "music that is uneasy and anxious with regards to society, our government, technology, the general direction of the world" is *Kid A*, the band's fourth LP, released in 2000.

Kid A was the first Radiohead album to top the charts in the United States, and in Britain—where the band had initially struggled to find an audience, even as "Creep" made them stars in the States in the early '90s—it went platinum within just one week. *Kid A* later won a Grammy for Best Alternative Album, along with garnering a nomination for one of the night's top honors, Album of the Year. It was the band's second nod in that category, after *OK Computer* in 1998.

In time, *Kid A* would come to be regarded as one of the best albums of the aughts, and then a defining record of the early twenty-first century. Even as rock music receded from the mainstream of music culture, *Kid A* remained one of the only rock records to be considered truly important, a landmark touchstone for the modern era.

And yet these statistics and accolades belie what was, in the fall of 2000, a highly contentious release. *Kid A* was Radiohead's grand digression from the guitar-rock splendor of their previous two albums, 1995's *The Bends* and 1997's *OK Computer*. A chilly, insular work in which the band's melodic, larger-than-life dynamics were muted, and the catchy choruses were garbled like dial-up signals. A self-consciously "difficult" work meant to usher Radiohead into a new century, though it also struck many listeners as merely a pretentious, anti-pop provocation.

"*Kid A* is like getting a massive eraser out and starting again," Thom Yorke declared upon the album's release. "I find it difficult to think of the path we've chosen as 'rock music.'"

While critics were divided on the merits of *Kid A*, the passion of those who hated it outweighed the relatively cautious regard of its admirers. The most memorable pan dismissed *Kid A* as "tubby, ostentatious, self-congratulatory, look-ma-I-can-suck-my-own-cock whiny old rubbish." While other reviews weren't quite *that* insulting, the skepticism of music writers toward *Kid A* nonetheless was pronounced, and often withering.

Fans were also polarized. Some felt *Kid A* was a bold experiment that pushed Radiohead into an exciting new sonic dimension, while others lamented that the finest guitar band of their generation had abandoned what they were best at—stirring, arena-filling anthems.

What couldn't be denied is that *Kid A*, love it or hate it, was very much a product of its moment. It was the definitive musical statement about how it felt to live at the start of an uncertain new era, right after the end of an old, fraught one. In that way, it was tied to the cinema of the time. Movies like *The Matrix*, *Fight Club*, and *Vanilla Sky* arrived between 1999 and 2001, and were infused with deep apprehension about modernity and how technology disconnected people from one another, as well as a core essence of themselves.

For those of us who treated the album as an event, *Kid A* signified a cultural turning point. Even if you didn't get the *how* of *Kid A*, you intuitively understood the *why*. It was a confusing album for a deeply confused time.

The anxiety at the start of the twenty-first century wasn't unique. In the late 1800s, the French called it fin de siècle, which translates simply to "end of the century," but more broadly describes the pervasive feelings of wariness and pessimism about the onset of the twentieth century. For citizens of the late nineteenth century, this ennui was driven by the changes wrought by the Second Industrial Revolution, in which new systems—including railroads and telegraphs—were implemented that connected people across vast tracts of land like never before, in a way that must have felt as revolutionary as the dawn of the Internet seemed one century later.

People in the late 1800s also felt unmoored by works of scientific scholarship like *On the Origin of Species*, Charles Darwin's 1859 book postulating that evolution, and not God, was the guiding force of the human race. What if God . . . wasn't real? What, then, was the point of life? Was there a point at all? If we are really just semi-intelligent beings descended from monkeys, what makes *us* special?

Numerous religions historically had already attached apocalyptic significance to the end of a millennium, believing it was a time of judgment and deliverance. But the sense that foundational ideologies, if not an entire way of life, were in the process of being dismantled as the year 1900 loomed must have felt overwhelming. What could possibly lie ahead?

Everything, all of a sudden, was not in its right place.

The artists of the time put these collective worries into their work. One of them was a twentysomething English writer who wrote prolifically in a number of genres and styles. Though in time, H. G. Wells would become known as one of the early progenitors of science fiction. In 1895, he serialized one of his most famous stories, *The Time Machine*, about a scientist who travels to the year 802,701 and discovers that society has been divided into a rich class of pampered and innocuous creatures called the Eloi and a subterranean group of ill-mannered and impoverished monsters called the Morlocks.

In the manner of all classic science fiction, *The Time Machine* was actually a commentary on the present, reflecting Wells's socialist critique of how industrialism and emerging technologies were dehumanizing the populace, deadening their souls as they robbed them of dignity and agency. It proved to be influential in the "Dying Earth" genre of sci-fi, preoccupied with end-times stories about how modern-day dysfunction eventually leads to Armageddon in the distant (though sometimes not-so-distant) future.

We never tire of telling ourselves these stories as we fret about our own destinies. For rock fans who came of age during the first two decades of the twenty-first century, *Kid A* was our version of this ancient, recurring narrative. A forward-thinking work that at some point stopped being about the future as it gradually came to strongly evoke everything vital and terrifying and unknowable about *now*.

When I think back to the release of *Kid A*, what once was up is now down. In 2000, record labels still cared about selling physical CDs by a rock band, and the Internet was a utopian place in which fans gathered to share esoteric music. As for Thom Yorke and his compatriots, they seemed to be leading the charge for a new kind of music that would finally bury classic rock.

Two decades later, the opposite of all these things is true. The record industry has all but given up on physical sales, in order to focus on streaming. The Internet is oppressive, fostering division and inflaming entrenched resentments. And Radiohead is the epitome of an arena-filling, classic-rock band that was finally inducted into the Rock & Roll Hall of Fame in 2019.

How did this happen? Why did it happen? And what, exactly, *is* happening?

This book is a detective story. And like all detective stories, it is rooted in obsession—in this case, with an album that has remained a touchstone for members of my generation for two decades. In another nod to Raymond Chandler, this tale is also a bit convoluted, with three intertwining narratives that ultimately connect into a single plot—about Radiohead, the record industry, and the Internet.

Musically speaking, *Kid A* isn't the most influential album of the twenty-first century, nor does it come close to approaching the sales of the most popular music of its time. *Kid A* is not even the most beloved *Radiohead* album of the past twenty years—that distinction probably belongs to 2007's *In Rainbows*, the LP that was embraced by Millennials in the same way that *OK Computer* remains a touchstone for Generation X.

And yet *Kid A* transcends all of these trends and debates, because what it embodies goes beyond just music. In terms of the culture and mood of the times, *Kid A* is the most emblematic album of the modern era.

To explain why that is, we need to go beyond just the record. It's important to look at Radiohead's career before *Kid A*, and the band's path after the album, to understand that *Kid A* stands at the fulcrum of Radiohead's work. It's also vital to explore the state of the record industry before and after that record, and the ways in which Radiohead influenced the gradual shift from the physical world to the cloud. And we must also discuss the Internet, and how it has fostered the widespread communication breakdown that *Kid A* signaled.

Along the way we will celebrate *Kid A*, as well as critique it. But we will also revisit parts of our own lives that have since been lost—often without us noticing. Because as much as *Kid A* enticed listeners in 2000 because it seemed to herald an exciting, shadowy future, we keep returning to *Kid A* all these years later because it radiates like a beacon illuminating distant versions of ourselves. What is this record still trying to tell us? Maybe it's not too late to heed the warnings of *Kid A*.

Now, is it possible that I take *Kid A* way too seriously? It's not possible—it is *certain*. But I'm guessing you take *Kid A* way too seriously too. If there are thousands of other people like us out there, maybe we truly can pull something profound out of the fourth Radiohead record—about the band, our world, and *us*.

So, punch up *Kid A* on your preferred streaming platform. Push the Play button. Let that menacing synthesizer riff from "Everything in Its Right Place" wash over you. Detect the clutter of the multi-tracked, electronically altered vocals. Feel the tension rise in your body, along with (perhaps) a rush of nostalgia.

Pleasure and discomfort are now commingling freely. This is the past, present, and future coming together—your life as a pessimistic rock record laced with the hope of an escape route and the fearful suspicion that all roads ultimately lead back to captivity.

PART ONE
BEFORE KID A

The moment's already passed, yeah it's gone . . .

CHAPTER 1

TWENTY-FIRST-CENTURY OVERTURE

It begins one night in November of 1997, backstage at NEC Arena in Birmingham, England. In Radiohead lore, it is known as the Night of Thom Yorke's Fateful Mental Breakdown. But in actual fact, there are *two* mental breakdowns—one before the show, and one after.

The first one occurs after soundcheck, when Yorke—just one month past his thirtieth birthday, in the midst of the most professionally momentous year of his life—spontaneously decides to ditch the band's security and exit the arena, without informing anyone of his whereabouts. If only leaving Radiohead and everything it had come to represent in Yorke's exhausted mind were that easy.

When it comes to being an escape artist, Yorke is a hopeless amateur. A man who has spent the past several years inside the bubble of one of rock's biggest bands must *learn* how to disappear completely. But for now, the effort is what matters. His life is at a breaking point, and he's seeking the right metaphor to express his anguish.

You can try the best you can. The
best you can is good enough.

After wandering around the arena for a while, fruitlessly searching for an exit door, he finally makes it out onto the street. He sees a train nearby and decides to hop on board. Maybe disappearing completely won't be so hard after all.

I go where I please. I walk through walls.

He is a rock star now but not *that* famous yet—Radiohead's third album, *OK Computer,* has been out for about five months, and will be promoted with singles through the following spring. While the LP is a significant commercial and critical hit, the expectation is that the next Radiohead record will finally complete their transformation into the new U2, similar to how *The Joshua Tree* turned the young U2 into *the* U2. In this trajectory, *OK Computer* is merely *The Unforgettable Fire.* Grander triumphs loom on the horizon. That's the conventional wisdom in the industry, at any rate.

But for now, Thom Yorke hasn't been fully Bono-ified yet. Radiohead is still in its pre-imperial period. Popular enough to whip thousands of people into a frenzy while torches are lit aflame in the distance, à la U2's *Under a Blood Red Sky* era in the early '80s, but not truly massive in the stadium-rock sense.

And yet, on that train, the chances that Thom won't be recognized are close to nil. He is traveling in the vicinity of a rock show—*his* rock show—not long before showtime. Who does he expect to be riding a train at that hour? He has not thought that far ahead.

Before long, he realizes that he is surrounded by Radiohead fans. All he can do is hide as the train whisks him back to the place he just tried to escape. He has found his metaphor for fame—a closed loop of omnipresent discomfort, perpetual awkwardness, and inescapable impotency.

I'm not here. This isn't happening.

This is breakdown number one, the "lesser" one. The major breakdown, the one where "it" begins, occurs later that night, after a six-song encore that culminates with the climactic tracks from the two most recent Radiohead albums, "Street Spirit (Fade Out)," from *The Bends*, and "The Tourist," from *OK Computer*.

After wailing "hey *maaaaan*, slow *dooooown*!" for several minutes to a worshipful audience, Yorke walks with his bandmates to their dressing room. They should feel triumphant, but Thom is tired. Radiohead has been touring almost constantly for six months, and they have another five months to go. By the time the promotional march finally wraps in the middle of 1998, they will have performed nearly 700 concerts in the past seven years. In

1995 alone, they lodged 179 shows—essentially a gig every other day, somewhere in the world, flogging "Fake Plastic Trees" at the local neighborhood House of Blues, over and over again.

Something inside of Thom Yorke finally snaps. He can't speak. His bandmates, Ed, Jonny, Colin, Phil—all of his mates from long before the time that he was "MTV famous"—ask if he's all right. Yorke can tell they are speaking to him, but he can't hear what they're saying or respond. For a moment he's just . . . *blank*, like a catastrophically malfunctioning hard drive.

This might seem like a melodramatic, even ridiculous, reaction to being thrust to the top of the rock 'n' roll heap. But consider how others have reacted in similar circumstances. Bob Dylan crashed his motorcycle, rock–conspiracy theorists believe, in order to escape the endless, drug-fueled touring of his *Blonde on Blonde* period in 1966. David Bowie killed off Ziggy Stardust at a "retirement" show in 1973. Kurt Cobain tried to actually kill himself while in the midst of a miserable European tour in 1994, before finally finishing the awful deed that spring back home in Seattle. Relative to those rock stars, Yorke affecting catatonia seems reasonable.

I have seen too much. I haven't seen
enough. You haven't seen it.

He hates being on the road. He hates himself for hating being on the road. He hates that he worked so hard and for so long to put himself in exactly this position and yet he can't enjoy it. When Thom Yorke was a boy, he saw Queen guitarist Brian May on television and decided that he was going to be a rock star. By age eleven, he joined his first band and started writing songs. By 1985, he was leading On a Friday, the band that became Radiohead. And he just kept on going, straight to that dressing room backstage at NEC Arena, where he finally realizes that he got what he wanted but lost what he had.

In the future, Radiohead will be known as the band that doesn't have to show up for things. They will be inducted into the Rock & Roll Hall of Fame and Thom Yorke won't show up because of a scheduling conflict with the debut of a piano piece he wrote for the Paris Philharmonic—which occurred nine days *after* the induction ceremony, which amounts to a scheduling conflict only if you live in the age of covered wagons.

You know the phrase "fuck-you money"? Radiohead will one day have "fuck-you" credibility.

But in 1997, Radiohead still plays the game. Thom Yorke has been playing it for most of his life, starting with that bolt of lightning from Brian May's Red Special guitar. He wanted, for a long time, to be *the guy*. He had the same ambition and drive shared by everyone who ends up holding a guitar on television and inspiring the next generation of Thoms to become rock stars.

After "Creep" became a hit in America in 1993—it took longer for Radiohead to break through at home in England, where they started as an afterthought and laughingstock amid a now-forgotten generation of Britpop shooting stars—they did anything and everything to maintain their momentum. They played late-night talk shows and awful British award programs and MTV beach houses. They made corny music videos and spoke with reporters from Podunk newspapers in nowhere towns and pressed the flesh and kissed the babies.

And it worked. It worked! It worked?

Did it really work the way he wanted it to?

"I always assumed that it was going to answer something—fill a gap," Yorke said many years later. "I was so driven for so long, like a fucking animal, and then I woke up one day and someone had given me a little gold plate for OK Computer and I couldn't deal with it for ages."

We're not scaremongering. This
is really happening.

Once Radiohead gets off the road, Thom Yorke doesn't crash his motorcycle or blow his head off. That's the good news. The bad news is that he feels spiritually and creatively spent. He will decide that guitar-based music is dead, and that Radiohead is woefully out of step for putting out the album that supposedly "saved" rock.

He will buy the entire back catalogue for Warp Records, an electronic music label known for putting out records by cutting-edge, forward-looking acts like Aphex Twin, Autechre, and Boards of Canada. (This is years before streaming, and right before Napster made stealing music online convenient. Thom Yorke had to invest actual money in the sound of his future.) He finds that this cold, mechanical music makes him feel alive again, giving him the same emotional connection that guitars once did. He is sick of melody. All he wants is rhythm.

He also likes that nothing in his new record collection has vocals. He is dreadfully tired of his own voice—the plaintive purity of his instrument bugs him, and it will only get worse once he hears his voice come out of other singers.

During the summer and fall of 1998, as Yorke suffers in private, an affable Scottish band named Travis convenes with the unofficial "sixth" member of Radiohead, producer Nigel Godrich, to record *The Man Who*. Travis's 1997 debut, *Good Feeling*, was an undistinguished stab at nicking the classic lad-rock sound of Oasis's mid-'90s zenith, which already seemed like a distant memory in the wake of their coked-out and overblown third album, 1997's *Be Here Now*.

For the second LP, Travis decided to change course. They weren't a great band, but they did have one great idea: Rewrite "Don't Look Back in Anger" over and over, and outfit their luminous ballads with the delectable guitar tones associated with Radiohead's twin mid-'90s classics, *The Bends* and *OK Computer*. Who better to help them than Godrich, the man who helped to make those records?

But this is a mere preamble to the band that will come to overshadow Radiohead commercially and assume the "new U2" mantle that Thom Yorke has decided to forsake. In May of 1998, five hundred copies of the debut EP by a new band made up of London college students, Coldplay, will be pressed and mostly given away for free to record companies. Like *The Man Who*, it sounds like *The Bends*, and it's perfect for those who wish Radiohead still sounded like *The Bends*. By early 1999, Coldplay will sign a five-album deal with Parlophone, Radiohead's label. The year after that, they will already be well on their way to becoming one of the biggest bands in the world. Eventually, their popularity will dwarf Radiohead's.

Now that his old songs have become their own genre of British rock, Yorke finds that he can't write Radiohead songs himself—not anything that he likes anyway. He writes and writes and writes, but he can't tell if any of his words are good. He can't even pick up a guitar without feeling like he's dying inside. New Year's Eve '98 is one of his lowest points. In January, Radiohead is supposed to go into a studio in Paris to start work on the follow-up to *OK Computer*, and he doesn't have any material to show them. He wonders if he's going crazy.

Light another candle. Release me.

Paris proves to be a disaster. Radiohead works on a tune called "Lost at Sea" that had emerged during soundchecks at the end of the *OK Computer* tour. As a song, it quickly goes nowhere; as a metaphor for the new album, it's obvious to the point of causing acute pain. (It will eventually be given a new title that also describes the state of Thom Yorke and Radiohead at this time, "In Limbo.")

In March, there are more sessions in Copenhagen. Yorke still can't complete any of his songs. He brings in demos inspired by Aphex Twin and Autechre—typically a rhythm track spiked with a curious, noisy splat. Nothing resembling an actual song, and certainly not anything that a three-guitar band can play. Ed O'Brien, the handsome, dope-smoking guitar player, thinks to himself that the best thing Radiohead can do now is revert to snappy, straightforward rock. He's "fed up with prog-rock analogies" and the ponderousness of *OK Computer*, so why not try to out-Travis Travis?

O'Brien isn't alone. Colin Greenwood privately worries that Yorke might be leading them toward "some awful art-rock nonsense just for its own sake, so that it looks like you're cutting your nose off to spite your face," as he later admits in an interview.

Radiohead spends two weeks in Copenhagen, recording endless bits of music that Yorke insists will eventually be shaped into songs. He cites the great German experimental rock band Can, which would jam endlessly in the studio and then edit the hours of music down to the very best parts. Radiohead stacks their bits of sound on fifty different reels of two-inch tape, each of which represents about fifteen minutes of unfinished, meandering music. None of it sounds as promising as Can's masterpiece, *Tago Mago*.

More sessions take place in April, at a mansion in Gloucestershire, in southwest England. The tedium does not break. The band hates everything they record. Incomplete songs stack up like Post-it notes—there are as many as sixty of them, and Radiohead is convinced that nothing is useable. They tinker over and over with a moody, minor-key, guitar-based ballad called "Knives Out," which would've fit well on *The Bends* or even *The Man Who*. Later, it is reported that it will take 313 hours of studio time to record "Knives Out," even though it sounds (in the best sense) like it was gently worked out in about 10 minutes.

Radiohead is approaching *Chinese Democracy* territory. Perfectionism is curdling into toxicity. There's even talk of disbanding if they can't find a way out of the mania.

Yorke buys a Yamaha grand piano and installs it at his new house in Cornwall. For a few months, he follows a routine: he walks out on the cliffs by his home with a sketchbook, and he plays that piano. He sucks at it, but he finds his limitations inspiring. Gradually, he reconnects with his muse. He writes a song inspired by that night in Birmingham, at the NEC Arena, when he realized that he was now living in the future that he had always dreamed about, and found that it was his own private hell.

Well, at least one crucial lyric refers to that night—the rest are deliberately disjointed and obscure, seemingly put together at random. He does not want this song to include a trail of bread crumbs that the media can use to trace back to his own life. His words are jumbled, meaningless scraps of data, nothing more.

He plays the song for Godrich, who is not overly enamored with what he hears. A slow piano ballad with murky lyrics isn't exactly the lifeline that Radiohead has been seeking. Yorke and Godrich then decide to play it on a Prophet-5 synthesizer, with Jonny Greenwood manipulating the sound of Yorke's dulcet voice into a garbled cyborg whisper with a Kaoss Pad, an audio effects unit newly introduced by the Japanese company Korg in the middle of Radiohead's round of marathon album sessions in 1999. A new toy that produces an entirely new, alien sound.

The song is *the* breakthrough. Radiohead knows it will be the first track on the new album, even though most of the band doesn't play on it. (For a time, they decide to put it out as the album's first single. Then, they opt to not put out *any* singles.) The band members have accepted that they can now contribute by *not* contributing, when the circumstances call for it.

From there, Radiohead proceeds to record not one but two full albums. The first, *Kid A*, comes out in October of 2000. The first song, "Everything in Its Right Place," confounds listeners and critics. It doesn't sound like *OK Computer*; it's more like gibberish.

Thom Yorke is annoyed by this reaction . . . even if, on some level, it was precisely the response he was seeking. In the media, he retells the story about his post-show breakdown in Birmingham. He explains that the song's most quoted line—"yesterday I woke up sucking a lemon"—refers to the death-mask grimace he held on his face during the relentless tour cycles that Radiohead endured during *The Bends* and *OK Computer*.

He now chides himself for playing the victim back then, believing now that he abdicated responsibility for his own well-being. Making *Kid A* was part of rectifying those oversights. He had been stuck for years down in a hole, but he is out now.

Howling down the chimney. Release me.

In the future, Thom Yorke will be vindicated. By the end of the aughts, *Kid A* will be regarded by many as the best album of the twenty-first century's first decade. In 2011, the American electronic music producer Derek Vincent Smith, known as Pretty Lights, will create a popular mash-up that melds "Everything in Its Right Place" with Nirvana's "All Apologies" and Nine Inch Nails' "Closer," unofficially confirming *Kid A*'s status as classic rock for Millennials. Five years after that, "Everything in Its Right Place" will appear in the trailer for a movie in which Ben Affleck stars as an autistic math genius who is also a cold-blooded professional killer, confirming that Radiohead has ascended to "thinking-man's Smash Mouth" status.

When people hear "Everything in Its Right Place" in the future, it won't sound alien or cold or difficult; it will evoke glitchy cell reception and patchy Wi-Fi and decontextualized social-media updates and the modern reality of omnipresent technological interconnectivity at the expense of genuine human connection. It will eventually seem *logical*—even the parts that aren't supposed to seem logical. It will sound like screaming at your neighbors and never being heard, in an online landscape that is as dark, disorderly, and foreboding as a Stanley Donwood album cover. Or as inescapable as an arena you can't ever leave. In time, many of us will feel like the singer in the successful rock band—surrounded by every convenience, and yet thoroughly alienated by this supposedly inviting world.

What is that you tried to say? What
was that you tried to say . . .

I can't remember the last time I played *Kid* A, perhaps because I've never actually *stopped* playing it.

It's one of those albums that's permanently lodged into my brain, where it just spins on a loop. Sometimes it comes through loud and clear, where I can feel every blip, skronk, and digitally distorted vocal. Other times, it plays on a low hum, following me like a shadow, like how the string section stalks Thom Yorke in "How to Disappear Completely."

Let's quickly recite the track listing for *Kid* A like bros quoting the Dude at a *Big Lebowski* convention.

TRACK 1: "Everything in Its Right Place." Evil synths. Tasty lemons. Maybe the greatest opening track ever.

TRACK 2: "Kid A." A robot ballet on the moon. I heard this song a hundred times before I looked up the lyrics and realized that Thom Yorke is singing, "The rats and children follow me out of town / the rats and children follow me out of town / come on, kids." Yorke sounds like he's singing while inside the Red Room from *Twin Peaks*—his voice is treated in such a way that it's as if he's speaking backward, though he's actually not. Follow him through the album's dark portal, kids.

TRACK 3: "The National Anthem." The free-jazz one. The track you played for your Radiohead-hating friends to prove "they could rock." (This never worked.)

TRACK 4: "How to Disappear Completely." The one that could've been on *OK Computer* . . . if Scott Walker had produced it.

TRACK 5: "Treefingers." The interstitial one. If this was the first *Kid A* track you illegally downloaded when the album leaked, you were very confused, and then extremely pissed.

TRACK 6: "Optimistic." My first favorite *Kid A* track, because it sounded like my favorite tracks from older Radiohead albums.

TRACK 7: "In Limbo." My current favorite *Kid A* track, because it sounds like nothing on any other Radiohead album.

TRACK 8: "Idioteque." The showstopper, and the only track that can be credibly described as "electronic," even though *Kid A* is routinely described as an "electronic" album.

TRACK 9: "Morning Bell." The only track on *Kid A* you could possibly have sex to, even if the rhythm might accidentally knock your hips out of joint.

TRACK 10: "Motion Picture Soundtrack." The closing dirge. Funereal. "I will see you in the next life" is the final line. Thom does not sing it like he actually believes it.

TRACK 11: "Untitled." The hidden, additional track that rewards listeners who sit through the closing credits. What coming down from mushrooms at dawn feels like is what this song sounds like, as it should.

If *Kid A* feels like an ingrained part of my life, it's because Radiohead has also been there for most of my existence. They appeared to me at age fifteen, all because MTV put the music video for "Creep" in the Buzz Bin, a profound honor for musical artistes in 1993.

I loved "Creep" instantly, and I've followed Radiohead ever since—sometimes as a fan, other times as a skeptic, but always with keen interest and curious ears. It's a cliché to refer to a band or artist as "the soundtrack of my life," but Radiohead truly has been a kind of Greek chorus for my assorted ups and downs, supplying background noise to relationships, breakups, bad apartments, epic road trips, sleepless nights, and aspirational mornings.

About 63 percent of my life, to be more or less precise. As I write this, I'm forty-two years old, with a wife, two kids, a dog, and a mortgage. Virtually nothing about my life is the same as it was when I was fifteen. But if I were to somehow encounter myself as a high school sophomore, I know there is at least one topic we could talk about with equal enthusiasm, and that is Radiohead.

The same goes for my twenty-three-year-old self, another guy who is now otherwise unknown to me. That's how old I was when *Kid A* was released. Is it strange to refer to myself as a series of other people who are essentially strangers? There's a myth that the title of *Kid A* refers to the first cloned human, which persists among fans even though the band has debunked it. Meanwhile, I can't help cloning myself, over and over, in my own mind. The version of myself who heard *Kid A* for the first time was my own Kid H or Kid I.

Thinking about *Kid A* involves reacquainting myself with the people who I used to be, as it is for all of us who revisit art that implants itself on our lives. Over time, our past selves slip into the space between memory and fiction. We know they're back there, but we can never be totally sure if what we remember is real. A classic album like *Kid A* can connect us with the past, present, and future simultaneously, making them feel like one and the same, a multidimensional form of historical and personal narrative.

In terms of *linear* time, October 2, 2000—the date of *Kid A's* release in the United States—is a very long time ago. Imagining what my life was like then is as strange and unfathomable, I'm sure, as it was back then thinking about my life at age forty-two.

I know how I felt about *Pablo Honey* in the moment, because I wrote my thoughts down as a junior rock critic for my hometown newspaper, *The Post-Crescent*. In a review dated November 24, 1993—about seven months after the album's release, because you could do that in a pre-Internet world ruled by daily newspapers—I wrote the following:

> When it comes to rock 'n' roll, I have a soft spot in my heart for bands that can write solid melodies and play those melodies with clinch-fisted [*sic*] intensity.
>
> Radiohead is a band like that. They are a new band from the U.K. Radiohead's debut album is called *Pablo Honey*, an excellent collection of rock-flavored pop songs.
>
> Radiohead has a sound reminiscent of early U2, with their dramatic vocals and soaring guitars. But the guys in Radiohead are not a bunch of copycats. Their songs are idiosyncratic, yet catchy.

1993 me, I must say, is pretty goddamn adorable.

I didn't write reviews of the next two Radiohead albums, 1995's *The Bends* and 1997's *OK Computer*, but I nevertheless have indelible memories of each record. *The Bends* was my "wallow about women during my junior year of high school" record. I remember going on long walks at night with my Discman, and listening to "High & Dry" and "Bulletproof . . . Wish I Was" on repeat, like a character in a retro '90s teen drama on the CW.

OK Computer, meanwhile, was my "get high with my friend Marc, who otherwise listens exclusively to Pantera and Sepultura" record. This obviously is tied to an almost comically specific memory—the third or fourth time I heard *OK Computer*, I played it for my metalhead friend while driving around in his truck one night. I expected him to hate it (I'm positive that he thought *The Bends* was music for Poindextery wimps), but I witnessed his mind get blown during the non-chorus chorus of "Subterranean Homesick Alien," when Thom Yorke sings "uptight" six times (though the weed made it seem like sixty times). In that moment, Yorke's falsetto hit Marc with the force of Dimebag Darrell's down-tuned guitar.

Weirdly, October 2000 is less accessible to me than 1993, 1995, or 1997. It's *blurry*, akin to the sensation created by the atmospheric keyboards that drift across your synapses like the last, early-morning remnants of an acid trip in "Treefingers." I sense the outlines of myself in the fog of that time, but further illumination remains elusive.

I know I bought *Kid A* the day it came out, as opposed to downloading it illegally. I know this because I *still* own it—thank you, physical evidence. And I'm pretty sure I liked it, though I'm also pretty sure I liked it less than *The Bends* and *OK Computer*.

There were other albums in my life then that I recall playing a lot more—Primal Scream's *XTRMNTR*, the Doves' *Lost Souls*, OutKast's *Stankonia*, and, yes, Coldplay's debut LP, *Parachutes*, which I declared was my favorite album of 2000 on some thankfully forgotten music website.

Other than the remaining vestiges of my CD collection, which has stubbornly remained a fixture in my home office even as I have embraced the streaming era with the rest of the world, not much else is tangible from 2000. The fact is that *Kid A* arrived right before the world as it once existed was consigned to oblivion.

For me, *Kid A* marks the beginning of the new century.

We all know that eras never start on time. Historians will often point to wars, national tragedies, or elections as the pivot points. The '60s, as we think of them, actually started in 1963, when John F. Kennedy was assassinated. The '70s commenced with the Watergate scandal. The '80s were kicked off by the election of Ronald Reagan, just as the '90s began when Bill Clinton took office.

But paradigm-shifting political events aren't the only markers of modern history. Pop culture also matters—it arguably matters *more*. Pop music, in particular, has long supplied handy signposts. Elvis Presley's ascendance ushered in the '50s. The arrival of the Beatles kick-started the '60s. The one-two punch of disco and punk defined the '70s. Michael Jackson's *Thriller* is quintessentially '80s, and Nirvana's *Nevermind* positively screams '90s.

So much of what would come to define the early years of the twenty-first century—9/11, the wars in Iraq and Afghanistan, the global economic meltdown, extreme political polarization, the proliferation of social media—hadn't happened yet when *Kid A* was released. The month after *Kid A* came out, George W. Bush and Al Gore faced off in one of the closest and most contentious elections in US history. In the end, the candidate who lost the popular vote, Bush, was declared the winner by the Supreme Court, the first in a series of destabilizing events that undermined the public's belief in justice, truth, even a shared reality. (*Hail to the Thief*, anyone?) Over time, the concept of alternate timelines coexisting in the same realm would no longer be a trope of science fiction—it would be a mundane tenet of daily life.

Millions of Gen-Xers and Millennials watched the fallout from Bush vs. Gore unfold in the news while *Kid A* droned on endlessly through their headphones. It was an eerily ideal soundtrack for what seemed like a darker, more foreboding time after the peace and prosperity of the '90s—a gloomily disorienting fanfare for a new era. Though we had no way of knowing exactly *how* dark.

No matter what the calendar said, it still felt like the twentieth century for most of 2000, especially when it came to how people consumed music. While Napster had infiltrated college campuses in 1999, unleashing a Pandora's box of consequences both thrilling (if you were a fan) and destructive (if you worked in the record industry), most of the general public still bought music the old-fashioned way, in brick-and-mortar record stores, after hearing about new records from establishment media outlets like FM radio and music magazines. Soon, the Internet would become the hub for music fans to discover, discuss, and digest music. Distribution would become more centralized, and corporatized, than ever—the Wild West of cyberspace would be tamed, putting "everything in its right place," as it were. In terms of our

IRL existence, we would all soon learn "how to disappear completely" into the digital ether.

But *Kid A* started out life as an actual physical album—a CD that you bought at Best Buy or Musicland, and then played in your car or living room on a bulky, multidisc changer. There was no Spotify or Apple Music. Illegally downloading songs was arduous and time-consuming. For most of us, the future hadn't really arrived yet.

Radiohead, however, was ahead of the curve. The band spent many months, in various studios situated in three different countries, battling creative inertia spurred by intense public hype, in order to create *Kid A*, boldly eschewing the classic-rock grandiosity of their previous work. Instead, they embraced a tech-addled and thoroughly alienated paranoia. As a work of art, *Kid A* arrived as a missive from an unseen time beyond the visible horizon, an inarticulate mishmash of garbled words and passive-aggressive electronics that eerily emulated the contextual wastelands of online communication platforms that were still several years away.

It didn't comment directly on the future; only one song, "Idioteque," can be credibly described as "apocalyptic," though the album artwork by Stanley Donwood depicts a dystopian wasteland devastated by fires, monsters, and climate change. But *Kid A* wasn't really all that prescient as text; the lyrics, by design, didn't actually *say* anything coherent. Rather, the entire package felt *of* the future.

Kid A embodied how things would eventually come to feel, look, and sound. The mood of ubiquitous dread and digital remove that the music evokes; the non-sequitur lyrics that double as status updates ("yesterday I woke up sucking a lemon"; "I'm not here, this isn't happening"; "the best you can is good enough");

and the overwhelming feeling that technology has interconnected all of our lives while cutting us off from our own humanity.

Kid A is a doom-laden overture for our modern times. We now live in the world this album foreshadowed. The question is, how did we get here?

CHAPTER 2

ANYONE CAN PLAY GUITAR (OR NOT)

You can put *Kid* A on now, *at this very moment*, and it will be brand-new for anyone who has never heard it.

Kid A also will exist ten years from now, as well as ten thousand years from now. And it will seem even more mind-blowing and otherworldly, as a missive from a lost, fallen culture. Whether anyone at that time will actually play *Kid* A, or be alive to care, is a different question. But the dinosaur bones of *Kid* A will be there to be dug up and studied for anyone with an arcane fascination with early twenty-first-century rock music.

For now, I'm not concerned with how *Kid* A sounds decades after it was first released. We'll get to that eventually. What I want to address *at this very moment* is how *Kid* A changed how Radiohead is perceived during the period *before* the album came out. Because *Kid A* now also exists in the fall of 1988, when Thom Yorke entered the University of Exeter as a puckish, ornery nineteen-year-old.

If what happened to Yorke later in life had never occurred, his college experience wouldn't be notable to anyone not intimately involved in his personal life. The band he formed with the other members of Radiohead, On a Friday, would've also been forgotten. If not for albums like *Kid A*, nobody would have posted On a Friday's demos from the mid-'80s on eBay twenty years later in the hopes of nabbing tens of thousands of dollars. The only reason anyone now wants to listen to unexceptional On a Friday tracks like "Girl (In a Purple Dress)" is so they can link the fumbling piano chords and clumsily syncopated drum beats in some vague way to "Idioteque" or "Morning Bell."

History has a way of retconning the future into the past. In our imagined daydream of 1988, On a Friday and *Kid A* sit side by side on the same universal plane. It's as if we're all living inside the Overlook Hotel from *The Shining*. *Kid A* is here. *Kid A* was *always* here. And it will always be here.

Thom Yorke was bored at Exeter. He had already put off college for a year, working odd jobs and playing an occasional gig with On a Friday. The band's first ever show, in the summer of 1987, was a thoroughly unexceptional affair at the Jericho Tavern in Oxford, a venue that would come to loom large in the early history of Radiohead. Jonny Greenwood, age fifteen and not yet a full-fledged member of the band, stood onstage with a harmonica while three saxophonists blared behind the band. Later, in response to On a Friday's first demo tape, a local music critic concluded, "It was hard work listening to this lot"—an early echo of the complaints made by many British scribes who were baffled by *Kid A* thirteen years later.

Yorke dealt with his collegiate ennui in typical fashion—by drinking and drugging too much. Sometimes, he would work himself up into such a lather with booze that it would fire up a new song idea. One night, he sketched out a tune about a love-lorn loser who hates himself so much that it curdles into obsessive, stalkerish resentment over an idealized object of affection. A guy who sees himself as a weirdo who definitely does not belong here.

What drove Thom Yorke to write "Creep"? He's never been all that forthcoming. "I wrote it at college," he said in 1993. "I wasn't very happy with the lyrics; I thought they were pretty crap." And that's about as articulate as he's been on the topic.

What we know is that Yorke was an Elvis Costello fan in the late '80s. He was especially enamored with *Blood & Chocolate*, one of two masterpieces Costello released in 1986—the first, the roots rock throwback *King of America*, arrived in spring, while the infinitely more churlish *Blood & Chocolate* came out about a month before Yorke's eighteenth birthday in the fall. It's not a surprise that Yorke gravitated to the unruly one. (Though Yorke and Jonny Greenwood did cover one of the best songs on *King of America*, "I'll Wear It Proudly," at the 1999 Tibetan Freedom Concert.) More than a decade later, Yorke credited *Blood & Chocolate* as "the album that made me change the way I thought about recording and writing music. Lyrics, too." You can hear that influence loud and clear in "Creep."

Costello famously claimed that his motivations for becoming a songwriter were "revenge and guilt." *Blood & Chocolate* takes that ethos as deep into petty grievance and fury as Costello would ever dare to venture. Written and recorded in the wake of an acrimonious divorce from his first wife, it's one of the angriest rock records ever made, a no-holds-barred exposé of male jealousy and misogyny that stays just on the right side of the reportage/glorification divide. Costello delves into the ugliest parts of the masculine psyche, but doesn't shirk the responsibility of making his indignant protagonists look like the absolute worst people in his songs. Time and again, he sets these vengeful recriminations to pungent, violent garage rock that veers wildly in and out of tune. It all sounds like a drunken argument that will eventually prompt the neighbors to call the police.

In "I Hope You're Happy Now," Costello whispers sarcastic taunts punctuated by sudden, jagged explosions of sullen noise. The guy in the song has been dumped, and he's saying all the right things in absolutely the wrong tone of voice. "He's a fine figure of a man, and handsome, too," he venomously mewls, with just enough hurt to implicitly acknowledge that his rival really is the better man. By the end of the song, he doesn't even bother to attempt to hide his contempt. "I know that this will hurt you more than it hurts me," Costello glowers as his backing band, the Attractions, slams into another car accident.

A few songs later, Costello descends directly into hell on "I Want You," a hymn to obsession so disquieting it makes you feel unclean for connecting with it. The opening line is chilling: "I want you / you had your fun / you don't get well no more." He sings like a man peering through a window shade at an unsuspecting victim, or an incel muttering to himself while staring at a woman's social-media account.

Actually, Costello doesn't so much sing as *pant* the song, affecting a breathy quiver that evokes peeping toms and serial killers in the throes of intense shame and heightened sexual frustration right before their cathartic acts of ultimate sin. The guy in "I Want You," again, is hung up on an object of affection—women are reduced to things throughout *Blood & Chocolate*—in the arms of another:

> I want to hear he pleases you more than I do
> I want you
> I might as well be useless for all it means to you
> I want you

But no matter how Costello frames it, a young man listening to *Blood & Chocolate* (like Yorke in 1986 or—about seven or eight years later—me) is prone to feeling empathy for the poor, self-pitying saps at the center of these songs, even one as broken as the person in "I Want You."

You can imagine how "Creep"—back when it was just a sketch, a mere drunken excuse to blow off some steam at Exeter—might have started as an attempt to re-create the claustrophobic atmosphere of *Blood & Chocolate*. It's the pathetic inner monologue of a weak man unspooled without judgment or self-consciousness, in a way that will strike some as ridiculously melodramatic and others as relatable, even righteous.

"Creep" did not belong here or anywhere for many years. Amid the On a Friday demos that have surfaced from the late '80s and early '90s, "Creep" never appears. It doesn't seem to have been part of the band's early repertoire. When Colin Greenwood, full-time record-store clerk and part-time rock-'n'-roll bassist, passed along the demo to an A&R executive that got Radiohead signed to Parlophone, "Creep" wasn't on that tape.

(The label liked "Stop Whispering"—a mostly forgotten power ballad that Radiohead hasn't played live since 1996—because it was reminiscent of U2's "Bad.")

"Creep" came out of a period when Yorke was woodshedding loads and loads of material that ultimately went nowhere—On a Friday didn't perform any gigs while most of the band (save Jonny) attended college, a break that lasted for three years. They hadn't played out much back when they were schoolboys at Abington, either. They would tape their rehearsals, play them back, and then rehearse again. "Nobody liked us except us," Ed O'Brien told the *New York Times* in 2000, around the time Radiohead reverted to playing out infrequently.

If Yorke's songs were mostly unloved at this time, "Creep" was among the least desirable heaped on a ho-hum stockpile. It was too personal, too direct, too obvious. In 1997, Yorke recalled playing some early On a Friday demos for a friend who complained that his lyrics "left nothing to the imagination." Instead of feeling offended, Yorke agreed. He resolved from then on to not expose himself quite so plainly.

Which meant that "Creep"—a song that tells you everything about itself the first time you hear it—must have seemed gauche not long after that initial surge of angst and alcohol wore off.

The story of how "Creep" ultimately became Radiohead's breakout song has been told so many times that it feels like a pivotal scene in a bad biopic.

Let's imagine Daniel Radcliffe, in a radical tour de force that will finally make the public forget Harry Potter, as a young Thom Yorke, who starts playing what he derisively refers to as "our Scott Walker song" in the studio while Radiohead is rehearsing for its first single. The producers, Sean Slade and Paul Q. Kolderie—both of whom are portrayed by Mike Myers doing an over-wrought Scottish accent, even though both men are American in real life—mistakenly believe that "Creep" actually *is* a Scott Walker song, which disappoints them, because it's the song they like the most.

Cut to the next scene in a recording studio. Radiohead tries in vain to nail a good take of "Inside My Head," another U2-esque number that only diehards will ultimately remember. It goes no-where. The Mike Myers twins suggest taking a stab at the Scott Walker number, just to loosen up. What they don't tell the band is that the performance is being recorded.

As Radiohead lays it down, the dashing guitar player Jonny Greenwood—played by Rami Malek, with the assistance of a floppy black wig and cheek implants—loudly checks the volume of his guitar during the pre-chorus, creating an instantly iconic "ka-chunk" sound. (To emphasize the enormity of this moment, the Hans Zimmer score swells uproariously when Rami hits the first "ka-chunk.")

Radiohead ends up capturing the entire song in one take. In the control room, they listen to the playback. "What do you think?" Radcliffe asks. "I think it's the best thing we've done in ages," Rami says. (This is the actual dialogue from the real-life session.)

In the biopic, the film would now segue to a montage of Ra-diohead enjoying instant fame and fortune as "Creep" storms up the charts. But it didn't actually happen that way. "Creep" didn't become a hit in the United States until the summer of 1993, al-most a year after the single first came out in the UK, in Septem-ber of 1992. At home, Radiohead was completely overshadowed by Suede, a swishy, swaggering glam-rock band in which every member had Jonny Greenwood cheekbones.

Oh, Suede. I am one of the few Americans who still remembers them. I even play their records from time to time. I especially like the first two LPs, 1993's *Suede* (the one with two beautiful androgynous glowing beings making out on the cover) and 1994's *Dog Man Star*, an overblown opus that's like Suede's version of *Be Here Now*, only with cocaine exchanged out for heroin. Suede was fronted by a guy named Brett Anderson, who basically looked like an artist's rendering of a perfect '90s British rock singer, with swept-back black hair, feminine, catlike features, and a look of perpetual insouciance. The "guitar player with mystique" in Suede was Bernard Butler, who resembled Johnny Marr if Johnny had tried to impersonate Jimmy Page.

In the early '90s, the smart money was on Suede to become the massively successful legacy act, and Radiohead to be the flash-in-the-pan one-hit wonder. But that just goes to show how stupid the smart money is sometimes. The British press was essentially forced to pay attention to Radiohead after *Pablo Honey* went gold in the United States in the fall of 1993. But the local press still framed them in the context of Suede, even though Suede's self-titled debut, the *New Musical Express* conceded, had been outsold 15 to 1 by *Pablo Honey* in the States.

Now the idea was to make Radiohead seem more like Suede, purely for the sake of satisfying the prurient interest of rock writers. Colin was compelled by *Melody Maker* to dish about his naughty collegiate past, in which he flirted with heavy drug use and homosexual dalliances.

All of this added to the disorienting feeling inside of Radiohead that "making it" wasn't worth it. Over time, they came to resent their hit song about resentment. While on tour in Providence, Rhode Island, in 1993, Yorke dedicated the B-side of "Creep," "Yes I Am," to "all the people who shat on us," protesting later to *Melody Maker* "about the sensation of being the underdog for so long, and how suddenly everyone's nice to you. And it's like, 'F you.'"

If people loved them too late in England, fans loved Radiohead too early in America. "Creep" translated to MTV and US rock radio because, unlike Suede, Radiohead wasn't ironic or androgynous or averse to overt rock-dude guitar riffage. For Yorke, it wasn't his words or his impassioned delivery that sold the song, "it was just that guitar noise," he admitted to *Rolling Stone* several years later. "If that guitar hadn't exploded where it exploded, there's just no way it would have got on alternative radio. And we wouldn't be anywhere."

And yet Yorke was still the face of the song—the freak, the loner, the alienated outsider. He was the one on the hook for interviews with middle-American Morning Zoo Crew disc jockeys who constantly asked him whether he was like the person in the song, and if he was just as messed-up as Kurt Cobain or Eddie Vedder. He played along, because that's what you do when you have a hit. But he came to believe that the radio played "Creep" too much, putting Radiohead in a corner it might never escape. "You can't imagine how horrible that was," he recalled in 2000. "And the thing about being a one-hit wonder: you know, you do come to believe it. You say you don't but you do. It messed me up good and proper."

"Creep" and *Kid A* now peacefully coexist in the same shared history—of Radiohead, of alternative rock, of all the people who have made those things pivotal parts of their lives. They're both trusty, reassuring warhorses. It's difficult now to understand how, for a time, they existed at opposing poles.

But Radiohead really was defined by one song for most of the '90s, and that song now has little to do with what the band's persona became. The cliché about Radiohead is that they make arty, esoteric, enigmatic music that willingly confounds listeners—and that comes from *Kid A*. But that's not how they were perceived before *Kid A*. They were pop music. A teen-angst band. Kid stuff. The sort of thing that anyone over the age of twenty-three reflexively scoffs at.

The specter of one-hit-wonderdom hung over Radiohead for years. In their reviews of 1995's *The Bends*, *Rolling Stone* and *Spin* framed their takes on how well Radiohead did or didn't move on from the ubiquity of "Creep." The *Rolling Stone* review, puzzlingly, dinged *The Bends* for being too poppy, harrumphing that "'Creep' whacked Americans because its message was unfiltered." *Spin* similarly dismissed *The Bends* as "never 'Creep'-like enough." This sort of reaction was inevitable for Radiohead's first post-"Creep" album. But "Creep" also appears in the first graf of *Rolling Stone* and *Spin*'s reviews of *OK Computer*. Only, in these reviews the tone is dismissive—"Creep" is no longer a standard that Radiohead can't live up to, but an albatross that can only embarrass them.

Radiohead continued to play "Creep" regularly throughout the '90s—356 times, to be exact, from 1992 to '98. But after *Kid A*, "Creep" rarely appeared in the band's setlists. At the height of the song's success, Yorke remarked that singing "Creep" felt like covering somebody else's song. Even back in 1993, the impact of "Creep" was so massive that it felt as though it belonged in the public domain. But by the early 2000s, Radiohead had truly severed themselves from "Creep," gifting it to the bizarre array of bands—everyone from Tears for Fears to Blues Traveler to Korn—that have performed "Creep" in concert in Radiohead's place. From there, "Creep" filtered down to *American Idol*, and then filtered again even lower down to the Ryan Murphy teen drama *Glee*. "Creep" has had a life completely independent of Radiohead, venturing to places the band itself would never go.

How do you escape an arena when all local trains will take you right back to where you started? For Radiohead, "Creep" was the trap and *Kid A* was the escape plan.

While nobody in the band has ever stated it in exactly these terms, *Kid A* was the album that kept Radiohead from being regarded as strictly a '90s band, like Bush, Blind Melon, or any of the other acts whose breakout hits are collected, along with "Creep," on the immortal CD *MTV Buzz Bin, Vol. 1: The Zen of Buzz Clips*.

It's safe to say that *MTV Buzz Bin, Vol. 1: The Zen of Buzz Clips* doesn't have the stature of *Kid A* as an era-defining masterpiece. But if you're looking for a snapshot of what rock music sounded like at the height of alt-rock radio, *The Zen of Buzz Clips* is absolutely essential listening. It is more eclectic than you might remember—the MTV Buzz Bin had enough room for Danzig *and* the Dave Matthews Band. "Creep" is situated on the track list between "Low" by the smart-ass country-rock band Cracker, and "Cantaloop" by the English jazz-rap group Us3. That's where Radiohead landed in the early '90s—somewhere between meat-and-potatoes guitar rock and British novelty pop.

(By the way, "Creep" is not the best song on *The Zen of Buzz Clips*. That honor goes to "Hey Jealousy" by the Gin Blossoms, which contains one of the all-time great rock song lyrics: "Tomorrow we can drive around this town / and let the cops chase us around." In later years, the Gin Blossoms have occasionally put "Fake Plastic Trees" into their setlists as they've worked the county-fair circuit. Though the Radiohead song they should *really* cover is "Let Down," an epic '90s jangler worthy of one of the decade's great jangle-pop bands.)

No matter the greatness of *The Bends* and *OK Computer,* Radiohead's career still rested on a continuum with its debut album, in much the same way that Pearl Jam's subsequent '90s albums all can be framed in some way as a reaction against the titanic success of 1991's *Ten.*

Pearl Jam really is an easy point of comparison here. It's particularly helpful for defining how Radiohead put the Buzz Bin behind them. Pearl Jam never put out an album after the 1990s that stands apart definitively from the band's "classic" period. This is not meant as a knock against late-period PJ efforts like *Backspacer* or *Lightning Bolt*—it's just a fact that those albums didn't have the cultural impact of *Vs.* or *Vitalogy.* But *Kid A* mattered at least as much in Radiohead's career as *Pablo Honey,* possibly more. And then Radiohead put out another landmark LP, *In Rainbows,* seven years after *Kid A,* ensuring that Millennials would have their own Radiohead album as crucial as *The Bends* and *OK Computer* were for Gen-Xers. It's possible those same Millennials like *No Code.* But the relative conciseness of Pearl Jam's "relevant" era consigns them to '90s-band status, whereas Radiohead found a way, starting with *Kid A,* to be extragenerational.

In the 1995 film *Casino,* professional gambler Sam "Ace" Rothstein (Robert De Niro) refers to Las Vegas as a "morality car wash" for lowlifes and degenerates. *Kid A* was like that for

Radiohead when it came to washing away the stigma of once being an alt-rock also-ran. But this cleansing resulted in some collateral damage, starting with the reputation of *Pablo Honey*.

The first Radiohead album is routinely ranked as either the band's worst or second worst LP, along with *The King of Limbs*, which actually deserves to be considered the worst. As an OG "Creep" lover, I believe this development is unjust, though it's not surprising in the least. Much of Radiohead's career can be interpreted as an attempt to bury its platinum-selling debut.

The members of Radiohead started telegraphing their low opinion of *Pablo Honey* practically as soon as they were no longer required to promote it. In 1996, while lounging in San Francisco with Thom Yorke and a journalist from an online zine, Jonny Greenwood mused that "when reviewers [say] bad things about the first album, we just sort of half agree with them." *The Bends* meanwhile had turned Radiohead into "that horrible thing of a band's band, or a critic's band," he mused. Two years later, amid the glow of *OK Computer*'s rapturous critical reception, Yorke insisted that *Pablo Honey* "was like a demo: 'Three weeks, don't worry about it, no-one will hear it, it's our first album' . . . and then so many people bought it. We were still forming and didn't have any idea what we were doing."

Pablo Honey certainly was rushed, especially compared with the open-ended, marathon sessions that yielded both *Kid A* and *Amnesiac*. (Though Radiohead deliberately worked through *Hail to the Thief* in about the same amount of time as *Pablo Honey*, knocking out a song per day. That album's lead-off track, "2 + 2 = 5," also opens with the sound of Jonny Greenwood plugging in his guitar, which is reminiscent of that *ka-chunk* from "Creep.")

Moreover, it's *obvious*—like "Creep," *Pablo Honey* lacks mystery and ambiguity. Instead, Radiohead made a bar-band record in which the pleasures reside exclusively on the surface, hitting instantly upon impact. At that time, they didn't have the luxury of producing a "grower." They had to be liked immediately in order to survive. Fortunately, they were really good at being superficially likeable. You don't have to play *Pablo Honey* a hundred times in order to fully absorb it; playing it a hundred times might, in fact, make you like it *less*.

This, of course, is not the Radiohead way as we've come to understand it. Radiohead makes Profound and Important Radiohead Albums, not a hit single surrounded by lesser-known filler hastily assembled and then slapped on a circular piece of plastic. Profound and Important Radiohead Albums are serious propositions that require serious commitment on the part of listeners. You must be willing to put in the same amount of time listening as they did writing and recording it. Only then can you and the band together achieve *fully formed* status.

You can't enjoy *Pablo Honey* under these conditions. And that makes me sad, because I loved this album when it came out. I know I did—I have that review I wrote for my hometown paper as evidence! While I can acknowledge that *Pablo Honey* is not as good as most of what came after it, I didn't have access in 1993 to the albums that Radiohead would one day make, the *actual* 1993, the one without the retconned *Kid A*. As opposed to the *imagined* 1993 of my memory, the one cluttered with all that inconvenient baggage from the future.

When I bought *Pablo Honey* for the first time, there was only one Radiohead album, and no guarantee that there would ever be another one. And, at the time, it was enough for me. When I put *Pablo Honey* on now, I want for it to *still* be enough for me. Therefore, I have decided to listen to *Pablo Honey* from now on with the ears of my sixteen-year-old self. I will not judge it via the lens of subsequent Radiohead albums—I am instead tricking my brain into perceiving it as the only Radiohead music that I have ever heard. Because lying to yourself in order to once again enjoy albums you used to love is good.

How refreshing it is that what I've come to see as flaws have been restored once again as strengths! What was *basic* is now *visceral*.

Once I put myself back in the guileless state in which I originally heard these songs, *Pablo Honey* suddenly sounds like a gang of bros thrilled by the larger-than-life noise they have spontaneously whipped up in the studio. I can shout along with the choruses—"I'm not a vegetable! I will not control myself!"—and imagine striking back against a parental authority figure, even though I am now a parental authority figure. I can fantasize about this album giving me the power to strike back against the beautiful and affluent oppressors at my high school. I can listen to Radiohead and just dumbly enjoy riffs.

Pablo Honey, in other words, *rocks*.

Anyone can do this with any work of art. You don't have to literally fool your brain, you just have to remind yourself that you once had a different set of expectations.

In the case of *Pablo Honey*, I wasn't looking for "art" or "experimentation" or "challenging" music when I was sixteen. I wanted to feel better about myself and my lot in life. I yearned to experience an even small rush of power. I needed to feel like I had some semblance of control. My most reliable vehicle for achieving these ends was listening to rock 'n' roll at full volume on headphones, and *Pablo Honey* is the most *rock-'n'-roll* rock-'n'-roll record that Radiohead has ever made.

A year after I bought *Pablo Honey*, I became obsessed with another band from England, Oasis, who made their hunger for rock stardom the primary thematic concern of their debut album, *Definitely Maybe*. For the next few years, the members of Radiohead made it a point to publicly distance themselves from Oasis and other Britpop bands. Yorke once dismissed Oasis as "a bunch of guys who act stupid and write really primitive music." In another interview, he denied that Radiohead had anything to do with Britpop because "we don't really like cocaine that much."

This, again, seems like revisionist history. The members of Radiohead weren't much older than I was in 1993. Phil Selway was the old man in the group at twenty-six when *Pablo Honey* started moving up the charts in America, while Jonny Greenwood had not yet turned twenty-two. They were all young men in search of salvation, and "Creep"—before the song's success held them captive—delivered the very things they so desperately desired, even the less reputable stuff (fame, money, influence) they were later reluctant to admit that they had once sought out.

My favorite track on *Pablo Honey* is "Anyone Can Play Guitar," in which Thom Yorke sings about standing on the beach with his guitar while the apocalypse descends on London, and thinking only about joining a band when he goes to heaven, so he "won't be a nothing anymore."

I suppose it would be wise to read this song as an ironic commentary on rock-dude solipsism; the part when Yorke claims that he "wanna be, wanna be, wanna be Jim Morrison" probably shouldn't be taken completely at face value. On the other hand, the delivery of "Anyone Can Play Guitar" doesn't *seem* ironic, and Radiohead has never been a particularly ironic band. The guitars are over-amped and arrogant and a little show-offy, and the rhythm section practically swaggers—Radiohead approaches actual glam rock on "Anyone Can Play Guitar." It's basically a prequel to Oasis's "Rock 'n' Roll Star," with only slightly more shame.

A discussion about "Anyone Can Play Guitar" would be incomplete without mentioning Radiohead's infamous MTV Beach House appearance from 1993. For those who don't remember the details of MTV's annual spring-break coverage: Every year the music channel would devote a week or two of remote coverage to some college-party destination, hosting a series of bands at a lavish beach house. Normally, the MTV Beach House was a venue for artists like Gerardo, the hunky early-'90s Latin rapper of "Rico Suave" fame. But every now and then, they would host some horribly incongruous act who definitely did not belong amid the muscle-bound bros and string-bikinied babes.

This is where Radiohead comes in.

People always note the same two things about this clip: (1) the extreme weirdness of seeing Radiohead in the context of the MTV Beach House; (2) the fact that Thom Yorke almost died because he dove into the pool and was dragged down by his waterlogged Dr. Martens. However, what is usually undersold about the performance of "Anyone Can Play Guitar" is Radiohead's commitment to executing some classic rock-star moves. Ed O'Brien and Jonny Greenwood both prowl the small poolside stage like Pete Townshend in *The Kids Are Alright*. And Yorke, looking resplendent in his bleach-blond Kurt Cobain hairdo, affects a breathy vocal and mugs shamelessly for the cameras on the Jim Morrison line, before dramatically hurling himself into the pool during the song's guitar-screeching outro.

There's another interesting and frankly sort of weird premonition in Radiohead's MTV Beach House performance: it's reminiscent of Jeff Buckley's death from drowning four years later. Buckley famously influenced Thom Yorke's melodramatic vocals on *The Bends*, particularly the song "Fake Plastic Trees," which was recorded not long after the members of Radiohead saw Buckley in concert in 1994. *The Bends'* producer John Leckie said Buckley made Yorke "realize that you could sing in a falsetto without sounding drippy." In 1997, Buckley went swimming in a harbor off the Mississippi River in Memphis. He dove in wearing all of his clothes, include his Dr. Martens boots. Thom made it out of the water, but Jeff didn't.

"Anyone Can Play Guitar" is hardly an isolated island of sublime trash on *Pablo Honey*. Radiohead dares to go even dumber on "How Do You?," a laddish pile-driver about "a stupid baby who turned into a powerful freak" that sounds like the Vines or the Hives or some other forgettable garage-rock band that was on the cover of *Spin* in 2003.

And then there's "I Can't," my most precious Radiohead deep cut that apparently nobody else likes, including the members of Radiohead. They've played it only nine times, and not since October 27, 1992, at a gig in Leeds that coincided with the sessions for *Pablo Honey*. But they never bothered to trot out "I Can't" after the album was released, and they sure as hell never even considered playing it on any tour afterward. Why have you forsaken "I Can't," Radiohead? It's just such an infectiously corny pop song, like a reimaging of Swing Out Sister's "Breakout" that's only 10 percent gloomier.

If the transparent melodrama of "Creep" and *Pablo Honey* was a necessary device for Radiohead to get a foothold in America in 1993, distancing themselves from it just a few years later was probably also required for the band's long-term survival. The wave of alt-rock bands that followed Nirvana already seemed pretty played out by the time *The Bends* was released. Radiohead initially promoted the album with its most abrasive and least pop-friendly track, the sputtering and disease-obsessed "My Iron Lung," in which Yorke pointedly sings, "This is our new song / Just like the last one / A total waste of time." Radiohead's spin on "teenage angst has paid off well / now I'm bored and old," that classic expression of post-fame jadedness which opens Nirvana's *In Utero*.

If this was meant to disarm a skeptical music press before they pressed Play on *The Bends*, the gambit failed. *Spin's* Chuck Eddy was among many critics who were quick to lean on alterna-hit jokes. "This is one of those follow-up albums (like the last Spin Doctors one and, I fear, the next Counting Crows, the Offspring, and Blur records) that I always hope will sound like ten imitations of the one or two great hits of the band's not-so-great previous commercial-breakthrough LP," he wrote, "but instead just proves the band is afraid to be pigeonholed into the only style it's very good at."

In case the implication of lumping Radiohead in with Spin Doctors and the Offspring wasn't clear enough, Eddy added several more unflattering comparisons, likening *The Bends* to "Suede trying to rock like Sparks but coming out like U2, or (more often) that hissy little pissant in Smashing Pumpkins passive-aggressively inspiring me to clobber him with my copy of *The Grand Illusion* by Styx."

This kneejerk mockery of early '90s alt-rock—particularly the B- and C-list stuff that never transcended the era—always makes me defensive, because when *Pablo Honey* was big (along with Counting Crows and Smashing Pumpkins and Cracker and countless others) it meant the world to me. If I ever claimed decades after the fact that alternative music didn't seem revolutionary to me as a teenager, I'd know deep down that I was a horrible liar. Because that music blew my sheltered, small-town, middle-American mind back then.

The earnestness and extremely un-punk accessibility of those alt bands read as dorky just a few years later. But at the time it was genuinely thrilling watching guys like Thom Yorke jump into swimming pools, if only because he clearly didn't look or act like Bret Michaels. It was music that transported you from one rather depressing path to another infinitely more interesting path. Inevitably, you moved past that music at some point to something else entirely stranger and more adventurous, as the members of Radiohead themselves moved on to a more adventurous version of their own band. But I've never lost my love, or my gratitude, for those initial game-changers that bubbled up from the Buzz Bin.

When Radiohead entered the *Kid A* era, the members were questioning everything—the music industry, rock 'n' roll, traditional song structures, even the very definition of what a band is. They also sought to deconstruct their own formulas, attitudes, and ideas about what Radiohead was and what it could be. But they never really *stopped* being who they are. They couldn't. All they could do was try to hide it better.

Maybe that's why I can still hear the Radiohead of *Pablo Honey* in the band's subsequent work. They're still the band that relentlessly grasps for the emotional jugular, leading with the heart rather than the head, and putting ultimate value on what must be intuited over what can only be intellectualized. They just got better at not making it so damn obvious.

The trajectory of pretty much every Radiohead album that's not *Pablo Honey* is that it seems weird and alienating at first, and then gradually sounds more and more direct and emotional. Think of the first time you heard "Paranoid Android." The prog-rock excesses, the menacing lyrics, the epic length—it was all so strange coming after *The Bends*, wasn't it? Like something you would have to work hard in order to get. Now think of the last time you heard "Paranoid Android." Is it possible to still hear anything remotely strange about it? It's just a mass of swelling balladry and guitar noise, punctuated by some incredible, dramatic Jonny Greenwood *ka-chunk*. It's *Pablo Honey* with superior chops.

As for *Kid A*, that album no longer seems quite so weird either. Even when Radiohead consciously ditched guitars, they still viewed the music they made together as a means of surviving the apocalypse. Anyone can play guitar—or not. The path from "I don't belong here" to "I'm not here" isn't so far after all.

CHAPTER 3

OUR FRIEND ED

Radiohead's aversion to rock-'n'-roll decadence is—depending on your appetite for Mötley Crüe–in–'83 levels of backstage perversion—either the most admirable thing or the most boring thing about them.

Nobody in Radiohead ever killed a member of Hanoi Rocks in a tragic car accident. There are no mud sharks in this band's lore. As far as we know, no one has ever gone to rehab or even been put through a paternity trial. "I've never taken advantage of the opportunity of one-night stands. It's like treating sex like sneezing," Jonny Greenwood remarked in the mid-'90s. Assuming he's telling the truth, this makes him uncommonly decent for a foxy guitarist in a successful rock band. (The next part of the quote, however, makes him sound like a prude: "Sex is a fairly disgusting sort of tufted, smelly-area kind of activity, which is too intimate to engage in with strangers." It's frankly a miracle that this man went on to sire three children.)

Radiohead's stability is the most profound lesson it learned from R.E.M. That was another band who mostly behaved well during their thirty-one-year existence. (Peter Buck's misadventures with a bowl of yogurt on a British Airways flight being a rare exception.) Michael Stipe once said of R.E.M. fans, "We don't get groupies, we get teenagers who want to read us their poetry." Radiohead has always courted the same kind of fan. If you worship Thom Yorke, you're probably less interested in sleeping with him than explaining how the lyrics to "Lucky" sum up the most intense romantic encounter of your life. The thought of Radiohead trashing a hotel room is like imagining the pope autographing Mother Teresa's breasts.

Accounts of Radiohead's touring life in the '90s are so hopelessly chaste that the only remotely salacious bits pertain to the band merely being *offered* action that the members swiftly turned down. In 1993, the *NME* followed Radiohead to the United States, no doubt still smarting from the utter failure of Suede to seduce Americans with their blouses, pouty pansexuality, and Ziggy Stardust posturing. (By '94, Suede had already put out its "strung out on bad drugs and worse sex post-stardom" opus, *Dog Man Star*, right as Radiohead concluded the *Pablo Honey* tour and turned to figuring out how to make *The Bends*.) Now, the British press was stuck with proclaiming Radiohead the unlikely choirboy saviors of rock.

As always, Colin was the most eager to talk dirty with journalists, even if this particular backstage anecdote wasn't about him. "We did this gig in Dallas, and afterwards this beautiful girl homed in on Ed," Colin told the *NME*. "She said her parents were away, that she had loads of coke and that they could be back there in 10 minutes. We had a day off the next day and everything, he could've easily gone with her."

Clearly here was the rare person who wanted to *get* lucky with Radiohead, rather than just talk about "Lucky." If this story were about Jimmy Page or Freddie Mercury or Nikki Sixx, it would have ended six days later at a seedy hotel on the Sunset Strip with a laundry list of unmentionable accoutrements and a line of cop cars parked outside. But this was Radiohead, and the rock star in question was six-foot-five straight-arrow guitarist Ed O'Brien, so the ending was predictably much different.

"He didn't," Colin said of the "will Ed or won't Ed" scenario. "That's just so typical of the way we are."

I like this story not only because it spotlights Radiohead's resolute commitment to not acting like rock stars, but also because it confirms what for me has long been a self-evident fact about this band.

The most attractive member of Radiohead to hang out with is Ed.

During the making of what became *Kid A* and *Amnesiac*, Ed was the best friend for Radiohead's most hardcore fans.

From July of 1999 up through the spring of 2000, Ed kept a semiregular online journal on Radiohead's website documenting the recording sessions. In the modern era, when pop stars broadcast their lives on Instagram 24/7, keeping an online journal might not seem all that unusual. But in the hypersecretive realm of Radiohead, at a time when they had consciously retreated from a rock world that expected them to be the new kingpins, this was akin to snapchatting with an insider during the recording of

"Morning Bell." To this day, Ed's pithy journal entries amount to the most intimate portrait of the band's work habits.

As Ed tells it, Radiohead in 1999 and early 2000 was stuck in a feedback loop of inspiration and creative indecision, coming up with dozens of promising ideas and then whittling them down over the course of weeks into nothing. "What has been interesting about this is that for me this is first time I am aware of the cyclical nature of our behavior," he writes in the September 2, 1999, entry. "Patterns emerge. Today was much like a day four weeks ago. Things came to a head. And although you wish that there weren't days like this, it actually probably aids the creative process." The tone is light, but the desperation is palpable. (Ed signs off with a pledge "to swig back a bottle of wine" before going to bed.)

One month before that, on August 4, Ed worries that he and his mates are "going down 'Stone Roses' territory." The scare quotes are Ed's—"'Stone Roses' territory" is a unique kind of hell for a British rock band, referencing the interminable gestation of the proto-Britpop behemoth's second album, 1994's woefully mislabeled *Second Coming*. The LP was decidedly not the second coming for the Stone Roses—it succeeded only in derailing one of the most promising careers in the hallowed lineage of shaggy-haired English pop-rock groups.

"It's taken us seven years to get this sort of freedom, and it's what we always wanted," Ed writes a few days later. "But it could be so easy to fuck it all up."

In the following weeks, the clouds parted a bit. Ed was always happy to play "Optimistic," the most (only?) Radiohead-sounding Radiohead rocker on *Kid* A. It's the track that seems almost impossible to fuck up, though Radiohead apparently tried to do just that, futzing away with it endlessly. He was also hopeful about the progress on a track that didn't make either *Kid A* or *Amnesiac*, the future "Knives Out" B-side "Cuttooth," as well as another scrappy number, "Up on the Ladder," that ultimately wasn't released until the *In Rainbows* era.

He notes Jonny's suggestion that "You and Whose Army?" should be arranged to spotlight the guitar and Thom's voice until the grand finale, which is what Radiohead does on the version that ends up on *Amnesiac*. Ed also jokes about Internet rumors that Radiohead was collaborating with Godspeed You! Black Emperor. (In 1999, the only people who were online regularly were very likely to also be fans of Godspeed You! Black Emperor.) But this is all a preamble to yet another breakdown, the one when Ed will be driven to polish off a bottle of wine.

A lot of the material they amassed in 1999 sounded dead at first, only to brighten when they revisited it months later. One of the trickiest songs was "In Limbo," a woozy blur that they tried repeatedly to get right but to no avail. It was one of the first things they tried to play in early 1999, when it was known as "Lost at Sea."

The tempo is unusual. It seems to move at three different speeds simultaneously. The rhythm section is slightly ahead of the vocal, and the guitars lag way behind in third place. It's somewhat reminiscent of the great 1960s Texas psychedelic band the 13th Floor Elevators—nobody seems to be playing *with* anybody else, it's more like they're playing *parallel* to one another. This sensation is difficult to replicate in a recording studio, but by the fall of 1999, Ed writes in his journal about how the band had warmed to what had been captured earlier in the year in Paris.

Another pivotal digression from Radiohead's established sound, "The National Anthem," was also starting to take shape that fall. The track had actually started in earnest two years earlier, when Radiohead was recording B-sides for OK Computer during a break from the tour. While the track hadn't totally come together, they sensed that it was too promising to be relegated to the undercard of a single, so they socked it away.

Actually, the roots of "The National Anthem"—which for an extended period was known as "Everyone"—went back even farther than OK Computer. The song's beginnings extended all the way to the On a Friday era. Thom Yorke had written the bass line when he was sixteen or seventeen, banging it out against the clanging of a drum machine. As the Kid A sessions unfolded, the track was nudged in a jazzier direction, inspired by the band's shared fascination with the iconic jazz bassist and composer Charles Mingus. By the fall, they had decided to bring in a brass section to punctuate the chaotic groove, a move that seems less radical when you consider the sax-heavy origins of On a Friday.

While Jonny Greenwood wrote a rough score for the brass players, Yorke coached them up. "On the day I said to them, 'You know when you've been in a traffic jam for four hours and if someone says the wrong thing to you, you'll just kill 'em, you'll fucking snap and probably throttle them?" Yorke recalled to Juice magazine. "I wanted them to play like that, like, this fucking close to going off, lynching or killing, it's like a mob just about to spark off."

Yorke and Greenwood proceeded to act as conductors, though they were really acting more as instigators for a musical brawl. Yorke got so worked up that he actually broke his foot from jumping up and down so much.

"The bit at the end was my favorite bit, because they said, 'Well, what are we going to do at the end?' And I said, 'I'll go,

1-2-3-4 and you just hit whatever note's in your head as loud as you possibly can,'" Yorke recalled. "And that was just the best sound you've ever heard!"

The most radical departure—and the song that most resembles the Warp Records catalogue that so enamored Yorke at the time—also emerged in the final quarter of 1999. "Idioteque" evolved from a fifty-minute improvisation created on a modular synthesizer by Jonny Greenwood that Yorke (and probably *only* Yorke) attempted to absorb in its entirety. "Some of it was just 'What?,' but then there was this section of about forty seconds long in the middle of it that was absolute genius," Yorke later explained to Terry Gross on NPR's *Fresh Air*. "And I just cut that out."

"The starting point for that was trying to build a drum machine out of very old-style synthesizers, kind of using the same things that I suppose the Roland technicians would have had in 1978 or whatever, to decide how to make something sound like a snare drum out of white noise and how to create the sound of a bass drum, a kick drum out of filters," Greenwood later explained on the Los Angeles radio show *Morning Becomes Electric*.

A central component of "Idioteque" was a sample taken from "Mild und Leise," an electronic music piece composed by Paul Lansky slightly less than thirty years earlier and released on an obscure 1976 album called *First Recordings—Electronic Music Winners*.

"We basically built a drum machine, and I played a record on top, at random, and had a radio playing, and was just trying to generate all this chaos over this drum pattern," Greenwood said. "And then Thom cut it into sections, and ended up having a sample of the record I was playing, which is this compilation of electronic composers."

Rise and fall, persevere and collapse, one step forward and two steps back. And then . . . a breakthrough. Noise suddenly blossoms into music. For more than a year, this was Radiohead's process.

Ed was the only man who could have provided this insight. He's the most outwardly friendly and down-to-earth member of Radiohead, the guy who seems most impressed that he's *in* Radiohead. He's also the most approachable member for the *other members* of Radiohead.

Back at Abingdon, Thom had propositioned Ed about joining a new band he was plotting with Colin, his former bandmate in a dime-a-dozen school punk band, TNT. While Ed is Radiohead's token jock—he dabbled in football and field hockey, along with being a standout cricket player—he also was a member of the school's theatre department, which is where he met the more outwardly arty and outrageous Thom and Colin.

Thom asked Ed to join On a Friday because he thought Ed looked like Morrissey, though Ed's resemblance to Morrissey hinges primarily on being a tall Englishman of Irish descent. Around this time, Ed also bought his first guitar. He didn't know how to play yet, but that didn't matter then. You can *learn* to play guitar. Kind of looking like Morrissey is innate.

Whenever you read profiles of the band, Ed is always game to analyze how Radiohead works in the context of other top-tier rock bands, an exercise that nobody else will engage with consistently. "I'm interested in bands as beasts," he once told *Spin.* "I'm interested in U2 and the Rolling Stones and Neil Young & Crazy Horse. I love the dynamic of musicians working together and all the voodoo shit that comes with it."

Admittedly, this is a big part of my own attraction to Ed. I am also interested in bands as beasts! Like all unabashed Ed people,

I fantasize about getting high with Ed and talking about legacy rock acts for hours on end.

No offense to Thom, Jonny, Colin, or Phil, but I don't think they would be nearly as much fun to hang out with. With Ed O'Brien, however, I already have a long list of conversation topics ready to go. In that *Spin* interview, he argued that *Exile on Main St.* was the last good Stones album in the context of arguing that *All That You Can't Leave Behind* is the last classic U2 LP. That's a three-hour conversation right there.

An important part of the mythology of *Kid A* is that Ed, the band's resident "rock guy," was the person most put off by Thom's push to go beyond the guitar-centric sound of the first three Radiohead records. This is supported by a profile written in 2001 by Nick Kent for the English music magazine *Mojo*. "My suggestion for *OK Computer*'s follow-up had been to say, 'Let's go back to the well-crafted three-and-a-half-minute song,'" Ed says. "I came from idolizing The Smiths in the '80s and I thought that would be the shocking thing to do."

Obviously, making a record that sounded like *The Queen Is Dead* was not going to work as Radiohead's bold artistic entrée into the twenty-first century. And this posed a serious problem for Ed, who could not simply pick up one of twelve other instruments like Jonny. He was one of the guitar players in the most transcendent English guitar band of their generation . . . and they were now making a big show of ditching the guitars. He went from being indispensable to being the *most* dispensable guy in the band.

Ed's solution was to make his Fender Eric Clapton Stratocaster sound like . . . *not* a guitar. A Fernandes Sustainer unit, a guitar modification similar to the one used by the Edge on U2's "With or Without You"—it's how he makes his axe sound like a high lonesome whistle blowing in the distance while Bono bellows about getting it all and wanting more—became a way for Ed to sound like he was exploring new sonic worlds on a synthesizer while actually tinkering away on his boring old six-string. You can hear it on "The National Anthem" and "Kid A," along with many other tracks on subsequent Radiohead albums.

The moment *Kid A* finally clicked for Ed occurred in January of 2000, when Radiohead reconvened after the endless flailing of 1999 in order to finally pull a coherent record out of their mountain of half-formed ideas and experimental whims. Nigel Godrich suggested dividing the band into two groups. One was to work in the studio's programming room, and the other in the main room. The idea was for each group to develop a set of musical sketches that the other group would then attempt to elaborate on.

Not everybody appreciated this brainstorm. The Greenwood brothers later rolled their eyes when a reporter from the British music magazine *Q* brought it up, with Colin offering a sardonic warning about Radiohead teetering on the precipice of "awful art rock nonsense." But Ed—who along with being "the rock guy" and "the resident jock" is also the biggest hippie in Radiohead—loved this exercise.

"You find yourself playing a Moog," he marveled, "or operating machinery that you've never used before. You're literally like a kid. 'I don't know how this works, but God it makes a great noise!' It was so fantastic to realize that that's as valid as playing a really great riff on a guitar."

Given that he's the only member of Radiohead ever spotted at a Phish concert, it makes sense that Ed is eternally down to jam.

This gleeful acquiescence on Ed's part was a crucial turning point not only for *Kid A*, but for Radiohead's survival during a period when the band's future hung precariously in the balance. As any Ed person will tell you, he is the most essential member of Radiohead, precisely because he sometimes seems inessential.

On paper, it's hard to describe exactly what he does. He's not the primary songwriter, like Thom. He's not the lead guitarist and arranger, like Jonny. He's not part of the rhythm section, like Phil and Colin. He is often called a "texturalist," which is a word guitar players use to describe someone who plays weird sounds instead of conventional riffs. But the term that most suits Ed is "glue guy." He floats amid all of the more prominent elements in Radiohead—Thom's soaring voice, Jonny's taut solos, the insistent snap of Phil and Colin's rhythms—holding them together without ever quite staying in any particular place.

In 2017, when Ed gave a series of interviews to promote his own brand of Fender guitar—I love that Ed still caters to Radiohead's guitar-nerd constituency—he never missed an opportunity to talk about Andy Summers, the unassuming guitarist from the Police. It's hard to imagine anybody in Radiohead other than Ed raving so enthusiastically about a band as uncool as the Police. These days, the Police is regarded as one of the passé staples of classic-rock radio, a dusty precursor to the jazzbo Boomer ballads of Sting's solo career. But when Ed was at that critical nexus point between early childhood and his teen years in the late '70s and early '80s, the Police were one of the most adored new wave bands in the world, and required listening for talented cricket players looking for "interesting" rock music played by men in short shorts and bleach-blond hair.

The track that most beguiled young Ed was "Walking on the Moon," a number-one UK hit in 1979, from the Police's second album, *Reggatta de Blanc*, the peak of the band's "fake

reggae" period. "Walking on the Moon" is a love song about being so elated after a kiss that you feel weightless, a topic that has
been addressed in precisely zero Radiohead tunes. But what Ed
cared about most is that ringing, recurring chord that Summers
strums right behind the bass notes, a spare yet epic sound that
gives "Walking on the Moon" its outer-space effervescence. It's
so powerful that Summers doesn't need to do much else—during
the breakdown about two-thirds in, rather than play a traditional
guitar solo, he just lets that chord ring for a couple extra dramatic
beats.

That was Summers's playing style in the Police, borne out of
musical invention and professional necessity. He was in a band
with two raging egomaniacs, Sting and drummer Stewart Copeland. So he had to let the bass, vocal, and drums take up most of
the sonic real estate on Police records, even though that's not how
it's supposed to work in a guitar-based rock group. Summers did
not play flashy leads—he played evocative rhythm parts designed
to spotlight Sting's plaintive voice and Copeland's hyperactive syn-
copations. The idea was to pull back while the bass and drums
drove the songs forward. And, for about five years, this unusual
but lucrative arrangement worked in the Police. Summers both
stayed out of the way and acted as a buffer between his headstrong
bandmates. (In the Police, "Don't Stand So Close to Me" wasn't
just a hit single, it also defined the band's interpersonal relations.)

When you listen to "Walking on the Moon," you can hear
what Ed O'Brien learned in terms of sonics and how to be in a
band. If Ed had a different kind of personality—if he were more
like George Harrison than Andy Summers—Radiohead would
have probably broken up by now. As the acknowledged power
brokers in Radiohead, Thom and Jonny had little reason to go.

As the engine of the band, Phil and Colin simply had *no place else* to go. Ed is the one member who might have had reason to become jealous, disillusioned, or eager to prove himself. But that never happened. Because Ed, the dedicated student of rock bands, realized that his most important job was to keep Radiohead together.

Don't think he's not conscious of this. "In a band like the Smashing Pumpkins, that kind of songwriting situation caused problems, because one gets the impression certain members of that band felt replaceable," O'Brien told *Spin*, offering an accurate assessment of how Billy Corgan's egocentric need for control undermined the band's unity. "But if you feel good about yourself, you will be honest and generous toward other people . . . As a band, we are all individually essential. In Radiohead, no one is replaceable."

The fact that Ed O'Brien, of all people, believes that is precisely what makes it true.

Kid A reinforced a narrative that's become a key stage of development for legacy rock bands—the pivot to "experimental" music that occurs somewhere between your fourth and sixth album, in which the guitar is deemphasized and electronic elements are prominently integrated. Radiohead didn't invent this move, but every rock band that has pulled this maneuver after them has, intentionally or not, evoked *Kid A*.

Let's address this issue the way that Ed O'Brien would, by looking at Radiohead through the prism of another long-running rock band: U2.

In October of 2000, Radiohead and U2 were both at critical junctures in their careers. That month, Radiohead put out their fourth album, *Kid A*, and U2 released their eleventh, *All That You Can't Leave Behind*. They appeared to be headed in opposite directions. *Kid A* seemed like a conscious attempt to alienate fair-weather fans, whereas *All That You Can't Leave Behind* appeared to be a transparent gambit to win back the people who hadn't bought a U2 CD since *Achtung Baby*. In time, both albums would come to be regarded as post-9/11 touchstones, though again for opposite reasons. Listeners discerned the bleak paranoia and disillusionment of the early twenty-first century in *Kid A* ("this isn't happening"), and they gleaned an uplifting message about embracing what really matters ("all that you can't leave behind") from the U2 record, which coincidentally featured the four band members on the cover standing idly inside of an airport, dressed in funeral black.

The first song on *All That You Can't Leave Behind*, "Beautiful Day," set the tone for the U2 record just as surely as "Everything in Its Right Place" acts as an overture for *Kid A*. After a brief fanfare of a ghostly synth figure floating over a drum machine, "Beautiful Day" explodes into an impossibly bright chorus powered by drummer Larry Mullen's reliable bar-band rumble and those signature church-bell guitars courtesy of the Edge. "Take me to that other place," Bono implores. "I know I'm not a hopeless case."

When "Beautiful Day" dropped in the fall of 2000, it had a decidedly different effect from *Kid A*, a record that confounded many more people than it thrilled. Cynics were inclined to hear "Beautiful Day" as a blatant attempt to rip off U2's own commercial high-water mark, 1987's *The Joshua Tree*. But anyone who could retain their cynicism after hearing that chorus probably never had the capacity to appreciate U2 in the first place. "Beautiful Day" was an instant classic, and easily the single most important song in U2's post-'90s career. "Beautiful Day" single-handedly extended U2's career another twenty years (and beyond), in the same way that "Start Me Up" gave the Rolling Stones just enough pop credibility in the early '80s to renew their relevance well beyond their creative denouement.

In 2000, nobody was comparing *Kid A* to *All That You Can't Leave Behind*. Radiohead had successfully put themselves in a radically different context. We were now eons away from Radiohead getting signed on the strength of demos that resembled songs from *The Unforgettable Fire*. Radiohead was now post-rock.

"Post-rock" is one of those terms that used to appear regularly in album reviews and is now basically extinct. Perhaps because *all* music seems "post-" a period when rock was at the center of music culture, and therefore worth reacting against. But in the late '90s, "post-rock" was applied to bands that resembled conventional rock groups in form but in practice strived to move beyond the clichés—guitar riffs, strutting lead singers, blues-based song structures—that define classic rock.

In a way, all of pop music in the late '90s seemed to have a post-rock attitude. It was probably the last time when reviving moribund genres of the past in an obvious and straightforward way seemed cool and novel. Basically anything that wasn't grunge felt fresh. People got really into swing revival acts and ska bands because it was actually interesting to like that stuff. Dudes who referred to their crummy studio apartments as "bachelor pads" got really into Brazilian music for about six months. Someone like Beck could play slide guitar over Dust Brothers beats and get hailed as a genius. Today, juxtaposition is the lingua franca of pop. But back then, it felt *different*.

My favorite post-rock band is Tortoise, a Chicago group that started putting out music in the mid -'90s. Tortoise played long instrumentals that relied on improvisation and drew from the same well of influences that inspired Radiohead during the *Kid A* period, including Miles Davis's fusion era, Kraftwerk, Fela Kuti, and Neu! The kind of music that record-store clerks and underemployed music critics hear when they die and go to heaven.

In the liner notes of Tortoise's 2006 box set, A *Lazarus Taxon*—album titles that sound like Emerson, Lake & Palmer deep cuts are a hallmark of post-rock bands—writer and musician Alan Licht connects the post-rock moment in the late '90s to the fall of the Berlin Wall and the end of the Cold War, "not to mention the commercial ascendance of grunge/alternative rock." He writes that these developments "set the stage for a new interest . . . in free musics (free jazz, free improvisation) but also for dub and remixing. The world stage was being remixed from an Us and Them mentality to a multicultural/globalist one."

He cites a Brian Eno essay from 1994 called "Unfinished," in which Eno argues that "we are no longer consumers of 'finished' works." On the eve of an age in which the Internet transformed everyday life, collapsing old media paradigms and flattening previously fortified walls between different cultures, Eno envisioned "leaving a world of 'know your own station' passivity," where "we stop regarding things as fixed and unchangeable, as preordained, and we increasingly find ourselves practicing the idea that we have some control."

"This was part of the incredible optimism of the time," Licht concludes. "A couple of years later Tropicalia and other Brazilian music was in vogue, the perfect sunny soundtrack to the late '90s dot-com bubble, anything is possible horizons."

Of course Brian Eno would come up in this context. When it comes to the "rockers who go experimental" trope, Eno is a central figure. The Beatles traditionally are credited with pioneering this concept in the mid-'60s, when they swiftly evolved from loveably mop-topped chroniclers of puppy love to acid-dropping sages drafting pocket symphonies that soundtracked the spiritual awakenings of Baby Boomers. But starting with his collaborations with David Bowie on the Berlin Trilogy of albums in the '70s, Eno has been the go-to guru for rock stars looking to move beyond rock.

He famously worked with Talking Heads and U2 on some of their most adventurous albums in the '70s and '80s, which inevitably inspired Coldplay to hire him in the mid-'00s. The surest sign that Eno had become a kind of "experimental" arena-rock cliché occurred in 2010, when the platinum-selling psych-tinged blog rock band MGMT put out its freak-out sophomore effort, *Congratulations*, and included a song literally called "Brian Eno."

Eno is one of those artists whose fame extends well beyond the reach of his music. Even his most accessible records—*Here Come the Warm Jets, Another Green World, Taking Tiger Mountain (By Strategy)*, and *Before and After Science*—remain obscure. But anyone who is casually conversant with rock history knows the bullet points of his biography. He began his career in the early '70s as the flamboyant keyboardist in the great English art-rock band Roxy Music, even though he professed to being a non-musician. As a solo artist, he named and popularized ambient music, which somehow made him seem both artier and more normal. And then he became the producer of absurdly successful rock bands.

Eno's most famous innovation as a producer is his Oblique Strategies cards. Developed in tandem with the British painter Peter Schmidt, these artistic prompts housed in a black box—like playing cards for pretentious people—are designed to encourage unique, indirect thinking in relation to solving creative problems. First published in 1975, each card includes a suggestion that usually can be taken literally, like "Use an old idea" or "Work at a different speed." Though some can only be viewed as metaphors, like "Gardening not Architecture," or as an open-ended idea that requires interpretation, like "Ask your body."

It all comes back to what rock bands are searching for when they hire Eno—to be freed from the sounds and rituals that remind people too much of who they actually are. Most of Eno's famous quotes are variations on the idea that artists have to break free from routine in order to produce greatness. "If you want to do something original, do something difficult," he once said. "I tire quickly of things that are too coherent."

What *exactly* it is that Eno does has at times been a matter of debate. He has occasionally been accused of being a glory hog, to the chagrin of some of his less famous collaborators. For instance, Eno is often presumed to be the producer of those Bowie Berlin-era albums, when in fact that role was performed by Bowie's longtime creative partner Tony Visconti. Eno was just there as a backing musician, cowriter, and muse. (Eno, for his part, never claimed to be Bowie's producer.)

As far as the cards go, they haven't always worked with the bands he's produced. Coldplay enthusiastically played along when they worked with Eno on 2008's *Viva la Vida or Death and All His Friends*. But David Byrne, who brought Eno into the fold of the Talking Heads for three albums starting with 1978's *More Songs About Buildings and Food*, was more skeptical. "If you already do that in your mind, you've got your own interior set of cards," he told biographer David Bowman. "You don't need somebody else's."

Another band that was eager to be guided was U2, who started working with Eno not long after he departed the Talking Heads in the mid-'80s. But the most Eno-y albums that U2 made were 1991's *Achtung Baby* and 1993's *Zooropa*, which signify the band's gleefully sleazy Eurotrash period.

In his fly-on-the-wall account of the band's historic Zoo TV Tour, *U2: At The End of the World*, journalist Bill Flanagan describes Eno literally directing the band during the recording of *Zooropa*. On a dry-erase board, he wrote the words "HOLD," "STOP," "CHANGE," and "CHANGE BACK," along with a list of chords. And Eno would stand at the board with a pointer, telling them when to switch up the song or play a different chord.

"It's actually a workable system," Flanagan writes, "but watching the thin, bald Eno use his board and pointer to direct a rock band is hilarious, like Ichabod Crane conducting the Rolling Stones."

Radiohead never went whole hog by working with Brian Eno on their "experimental" albums, like Coldplay eventually did. (Coldplay deciding to more closely mimic U2 rather than Radiohead is extremely Coldplay.) But they did utilize some Eno-esque exercises in order to inspire themselves. They worked on dozens of songs at once, quickly moving on as soon as they got bored. They put a premium on spontaneous moments or "mistakes" that might lead to unexpected discoveries. And during one of the worst impasses, Nigel Godrich made that suggestion for them to split into two groups to work on songs separately—which inspired Ed and annoyed Jonny and Colin.

"It's like you're dabbling, but at the same time, when something really comes off, it's all down on tape," Yorke said. "Nigel's really into the idea of capturing a performance, even if we're doing pure electronic stuff. So it's never like we just program stuff and let it run. There always had to be something else going on, processing in real time."

They also studied the bands who had worked under Eno's tutelage, most notably Talking Heads, whose 1980 landmark *Remain in Light* was a guiding light for Radiohead during the *Kid A/ Amnesiac* sessions.

In an interview with *The Wire*, Yorke confessed that they had quizzed Talking Heads guitarist/keyboardist Jerry Harrison about the band's methods during the *Remain in Light* days. "'Are there any loops or did you just play it all?'" they asked him.

"And they played it all, even though it sounds like tape loops," Yorke confirmed. "When they made that record, they had no real songs, just wrote it all as they went along. Byrne turned up with pages and pages, and just picked stuff up and threw bits in all the time. And that's exactly how I approached *Kid A*."

Zooropa came out in the spring of 1993, around the time that "Creep" was taking over MTV. Right when Radiohead was its straightest, U2 was at its weirdest—an inverse of the *Kid A* and *All That You Can't Leave Behind* parallel seven years later. Even now, *Zooropa* still sounds like a pretty weird record, especially for a band as massive as U2 was in the early '90s. The lead single, "Numb," is a monotone commentary track "sung" by the Edge about media overload set to a guitar riff that mimics a dial-up signal. "Don't move / Don't talk out of time / Don't think / Don't worry / Everything's just fine." It's the closest that U2 ever got to writing its own "Everything in Its Right Place." Even in the pre-Internet era, rock bands felt overwhelmed by technology-addled ennui simply from watching too much cable TV.

U2's transformation at the dawn of the '90s was not unlike Radiohead's makeover at the end of the decade. U2 was a European band that was closely linked with America after the mammoth success of *The Joshua Tree*, an album as emblematic of MTV-endorsed, mainstream-friendly "alternative" rock in the late '80s as "Creep" was in the early '90s. The album's popularity was so vast that it turned U2 into a caricature, a process expedited by the band itself with 1988's critically savaged (but in retrospect visually stunning and kind of underrated) documentary *Rattle and Hum*. In the movie, Bono wears cowboy hats and leather vests with no shirt underneath. He resembles a shorter and hairier Jon Bon Jovi. "We looked like a big overblown rock band running amok," he admits in the 2011 documentary *From the Sky Down*.

It was time for an "experimental" makeover. U2 absconded to Berlin to work on a new album at Hansa Studios, where Bowie and Eno (and Visconti!) made the middle album of the Berlin Trilogy, 1977's *Heroes*. For months, U2 jammed and jammed, trying to find a new direction. Just as Thom Yorke was obsessed with trying to make his band sound like Aphex Twin, the Edge pushed U2 to emulate the industrial bands and dance-rock combos he had recently discovered, like Einstürzende Neubauten and the Happy Mondays. Meanwhile Bono explored new ways of singing that didn't instantly recall his plaintive hectoring on *The Joshua Tree*, just as Yorke was obsessed with obscuring his own voice in light of his vocal style being reduced to a British rock cliché.

For U2, all of this self-conscious experimentation seemed like a disaster in the making. Occasionally, they hit upon a funky groove. But they weren't coming up with any actual songs. They began to suspect that they were finished. For a while, they turned on one another. "It was for a moment each man for himself," Bono later said, "which is a betrayal of the concept of a band."

It was the same fog that Radiohead was mired in during the making of *Kid A* and *Amnesiac*. You're trying really, *really* hard to come up with something . . . *different*. But everything you make just sounds like . . . *you*. And sounding like yourself is simply unacceptable. So you keep grasping for *different*. But what is *different* anyway? The problem with *different* is that nobody knows what *different* sounds like. And then there's the unsolvable paradox—if *you* are making something *different*, won't it also sound like *you*?

U2 and Radiohead were ultimately after the same thing—they wanted to be excited by their own music again. For Radiohead, *Kid A* started to come into focus when Thom introduced "Everything in Its Right Place," a song that sounded nothing like Radiohead's previous albums. For U2, *Achtung Baby* was rescued when they came up with "One," which would go on to become one of the big, reassuring archetypal U2 ballads.

When U2 struck out for the wilderness beyond rock music, their instincts eventually guided them back to previously trod ground. Their wiggiest experiment, *Zooropa*—the album they made with Brian Eno literally peering over their shoulder and instructing them on how to loosen up—came to be viewed by Bono and the Edge as an interesting misfire. A folly that directed them away from what they were truly meant to do.

"I thought of *Zooropa* at the time as a work of genius," Bono told journalist Neil McCormick. "I really thought our pop discipline was matching our experimentation and this was our *Sgt. Pepper*. I was a little wrong about that. The truth is our pop disciplines were letting us down. We didn't create hits. We didn't quite deliver the songs. And what would *Sgt. Pepper* be without the pop songs?"

"Beautiful Day," however, was *that* pop song. It helped *All That You Can't Leave Behind* sell 12 million copies, making it one of U2's most successful albums. When the band went on the road, Bono told audiences that they were reapplying for the job of greatest band in the world. The weird left turns U2 had taken in the '90s were now recontextualized as detours from the road that they were supposed to be on, taking them (to quote John Lennon) to the toppermost of the poppermost.

When Bono said that U2 was "reapplying" for the status of greatest band in the world, I wonder who he felt he was wresting that title from. In the wake of *OK Computer*, Radiohead certainly seemed worthy of the distinction. But making *Kid A* was a way for them to forsake the crown, and move in precisely the direction that U2 briefly considered and then rejected.

Perhaps Radiohead could sense that being "the greatest band in the world" wouldn't mean much in the world they were about to enter. Instead, they made *Kid A* for a post-rock century.

PART TWO
DURING KID A

This is really happening . . .

CHAPTER 4

THE BUTTERSCOTCH LAMPS

B y the spring of 2000, the British music press was getting antsy.

It had been nearly three years since the release of *OK Computer*. Radiohead hadn't toured in almost two. The level of anticipation for what they were going to do next was pushing already excitable English scribes to the point of hyperbole. "The time has come to forget Oasis, give [Richard] Ashcroft the elbow and even reject the adorable Embrace," *Melody Maker* declared that March. "If there's one band that promises to return rock to us, it's Radiohead."

The problem was that the members of Radiohead weren't all that forthcoming about what they were working on. So *Melody Maker* sent a reporter to literally wander around Oxford looking for leads.

This method proved to be surprisingly effective. The reporter tracked down someone from the Orchestra of St John's for an interview about recording sessions that took place with Radiohead six weeks prior, in February of 2000. It went down at Dorchester Abbey, a twelfth-century church located just outside of Oxford. You can hear the orchestra on three songs: "How to Disappear Completely" from *Kid A*, and "Pyramid Song" and "Dollars & Cents" from *Amnesiac*. Not that *Melody Maker* was privy to these specifics at the time, though they were able to report that Thom Yorke wanted "the color of the sounds being played to fit in with the mood of each track."

For "How to Disappear Completely," this mood could be described as "all-consuming dread that has been numbed to feel more like walking death." Superficially, it would come to be viewed as one of the relatively "normal" tracks on *Kid A*, a beautiful ballad centered on acoustic guitar that slowly builds to an operatic emotional climax, just like "Fake Plastic Trees" or "Exit Music (For a Film)." But what set "How to Disappear Completely" apart from those other songs were the string arrangements. They hang over the song like a cold fog, obscuring what you think is in the song sonically and hinting at other, elusive ambiguities that draw you deeper into the murk.

In his online diary, Ed O'Brien writes that Jonny Greenwood in early December 1999 had multitracked his ondes Martenot on the song, creating a sound that O'Brien likened to a "string section from Mars." Over the next two months, they tried and failed to "get it away from that band thing with an acoustic guitar," O'Brien writes, "which may have been alright when we were making *The Bends*, but let's face it has been done to death by both us and every Tom, Dick, and Harry guitar band." (This process seems to have to be spearheaded by the band, as Yorke later claimed that he had nothing to do with "How to Disappear Completely" after the demo phase. He wrote the song after suffering a minor mental breakdown over Radiohead performing at a massive concert in Ireland during the *OK Computer* tour.) Finally, with the Orchestra of St John's—as Jonny played along with his out-of-tune ondes Martenot—they were able to re-create that Martian string section effect, only this time with an actual string section that could achieve a truly enveloping, beguiling swell.

It's worth doing a quick aside on the ondes Martenot, an instrument that looms large in the legend of Jonny Greenwood. This strange device, which sounds like a theremin and looks like an ancient keyboard, was invented in 1928 by Maurice Martenot, a French inventor who played the cello and also worked as a telegrapher during the first World War. With that kind of résumé, it's no wonder that Greenwood was attracted to Martenot's namesake instrument. (If Martenot had been born in England in the late 1960s, rather than Paris in the late 1890s, he might have been *in* Radiohead.) Over the decades, he worked on perfecting the ondes Martenot, and also took an active role in teaching the first generation of musicians who attempted to play it. While his intention was to replicate the feel of a cello, the spookiness of the ondes Martenot's alien tones became most associated with film scores, particularly for sci-fi and horror flicks. That is, until Jonny Greenwood fashioned himself as the Eddie Van Halen of the instrument.

For the British music press in early 2000, the job of reporting on *Kid A* required more than digging up arcane trivia on the ondes Martenot. The mad pursuit for every scrap of information about Radiohead's mysterious new album mostly resulted in the sort of drivel that music journalists are forced to turn out when readers want content, no matter the lack of actual news to report. And yet *Melody Maker* was dogged in its pursuit of England's most reluctant superstars. First, they showed up at Phil Selway's house uninvited, and peppered him with questions about when the album was coming out.

"We don't even know when it's coming out ourselves," he demurred.

Then they went to Colin Greenwood's house. His girlfriend answered the door. "How did you know where we live?" she asked.

Then the reporter went to Ed O'Brien's house, and Ed managed to sneak into a car before being accosted. But *Melody Maker* was able to corner Plank, also known as Peter Clements, the band's longtime roadie.

"Is it good? Oh yeah, it's very good," Plank offered. What else was he going to say? "I'm reluctant to answer questions because I'm always getting approached by journalists," he added.

What's most striking when you read stories like this is that Radiohead still hadn't fully shaken the pop-group residue from "Creep." *OK Computer* had granted Radiohead a new level of critical reverence, but that didn't prevent journalists from knocking on their front doors and harassing their girlfriends in the hopes of hearing a loose bit of gossip that they could plaster on the cover of the next issue. They still were the sort of band that music magazines wanted (and, for the sake of reader demand, *needed*) to dish about.

So much of what was being shared about Radiohead that spring proved to be closer to rumor than fact. *Melody Maker* procured a CD from a so-called shadowy trader that was supposedly making the rounds in Oxford, purported to be a bootleg from the sessions. The article mentions "How to Disappear Completely" and "Motion Picture Soundtrack," as well as the elusive "True Love Waits," that legendary white whale the band tried and failed for years to get right. (It didn't end up on a Radiohead studio album until 2016's *A Moon Shaped Pool*.)

"Radiohead 2000 won't be making pop songs," *Melody Maker* concluded. "It's going to be orchestrated rock messed around with computers, looped and spliced adventures in sound, art rock for the people with funky jazz influences and white noise. Expect long, drawn-out experiments and beautiful journeys, with Thom's voice more intense than ever."

This was the narrative set forth for *Kid A* months before anyone actually heard it, and it's amazing how much it *still* informs how the album is perceived. Though when you deconstruct it, the classification doesn't really hold up to scrutiny. Is *Kid A* "funky" or replete with "jazz influences and white noise"? Not really. Not much beyond "The National Anthem," anyway.

It's difficult to hear *Kid A* as those in early 2000 *imagined* it would sound like. What is clear is that Radiohead's new music wasn't described in advance as an enticing or, you know, *fun* listen. Yes, it was "adventurous" and "experimental." And it was expected to change rock music forever. But there's almost a sense of foreboding in how many music journalists looked ahead to the next Radiohead record. It wasn't presented as a potentially pleasurable experience. It seemed more like work.

The British music press wouldn't get a real taste of Radiohead's latest songs until that summer, when the band went back on the road for about three weeks in June and July.

The highest-profile gig was on July 1, at Meltdown, an annual festival curated by a different musician or industry luminary each year. In 2000, it was Scott Walker, the laconic crooner who had started in the 1960s as a teen-oriented pop star and later took a dramatic turn toward difficult and deeply fucked-up art rock on albums like 1995's *Tilt* and, later, 2006's terrifying post-9/11 meditation, *The Drift*. It was exactly the trajectory that Radiohead was attempting to follow, from "Creep" (which was initially mistaken for a Scott Walker song by the producers of *Pablo Honey*) to *Kid A*.

Out of twenty-two songs performed by Radiohead at Meltdown, ten were new. They opened with the cascading guitar shimmers of "Optimistic." This had become the custom during the shows leading up to the festival. After two familiar favorites, "Bones" from *The Bends* and "Karma Police" from *OK Computer*, it was "Morning Bell," another relatively accessible song centered on a Fender Rhodes electric piano not all that different from the lick from "Karma Police." The most polarizing number from *Kid A*, "The National Anthem," came in the seventh slot, after "Talk Show Host," a B-side from the "Street Spirit" single that became a radio hit after it was remixed by Nellee Hooper and included on the zeitgeisty soundtrack to Baz Luhrmann's *Romeo + Juliet* in 1996. Then it was "My Iron Lung," which had once qualified as a "difficult" Radiohead song in the wake of *Pablo Honey*, and now registered as a comfy favorite.

Radiohead followed this pattern throughout the set: always chase something different with something familiar. A double shot of "You and Whose Army?" and "Dollars & Cents" is followed by a mini–greatest-hits valedictory run through "Exit Music (For a Film)," "Lucky," "Airbag," and "Just."

When you listen to the bootleg of the Meltdown concert, Radiohead seems pretty relaxed. Kind of remarkable, considering the importance of the gig and the fact that most of the audience didn't know nearly half the songs on the setlist. Perhaps the band was heartened by *some* people applauding as they went into "Everything in Its Right Place" at the end of the proper set, as well as by the warm response given to "Pyramid Song" (then referred to by the tapers as "Egyptian Song") at the start of the encore.

Surely there were hardcore fans following them from concert to concert. But live recordings of the shows the band played in Spain, Italy, Greece, and France that June had also already shown up on the Internet. Downloading those lo-fi, alluringly grainy live versions of future *Kid A* and *Amnesiac* tracks was the next best thing to hearing the studio recordings. Fans ate them up.

In the room, audience reaction to the new songs, judging from the tape, seems at least respectfully appreciative. Nobody is booing or expressing outward consternation with Radiohead's new material. This was far removed from a "Dylan goes electric"–type tour. The vibe is loose enough to allow for Ed to tell a story about watching a nature program regarding the mating rituals of chinchillas. The female chinchilla, Ed relates, will urinate in the male chinchilla's face in order to express her dissatisfaction. I've heard enough Radiohead live bootlegs to know that this is not the typical kind of banter one hears before they play "Paranoid Android." An all-around fun show, in other words.

But when you read reviews of the Meltdown performance, you get a different impression. Writers for some of the UK's biggest music magazines swiftly expressed their disapproval with Radiohead's new material. *Melody Maker* picked up its own "no pop songs" narrative from the spring and weaponized it against the band, expressing their bemusement over the "two hours of mesmerizing confusion" the band had supposedly unleashed.

The magazine sniffed that seeing Radiohead live "is the musical equivalent of [a] mathematical formula—mind-blowing once you get it, but hard work in the meantime." They added that "experimentation must be weighing them down . . . because it's not until they switch the lights on during cosmic tear-jerker 'Lucky' that we can actually read the emotion in Ed's face and feel fully engaged."

"We wish your new stuff sounded more like the old stuff" isn't the most forward-thinking of critical stances. But that was essentially *Melody Maker*'s position. (The best they could muster was deeming "Knives Out," a straightforward minor-key rock song that could have been on *The Bends*, "almost catchy.") And it was the stance taken by most other UK publications. "Many of the new songs betray origins as rehearsal-room jams—all looping basslines and unresolving riffs that meander rather than navigate surprising intervals," wrote *Mojo*'s Jim Irvin. "Perhaps they're wary of sounding too much like themselves."

The *New Musical Express* wasn't quite so scathing, though its dispassionate, almost clinical account betrays a similar lack of enthusiasm for Radiohead's new material. (The most interesting part of the *NME*'s review is the claim that Yorke effected "comically phallic gestures with his guitar" during "The National Anthem." Nothing remotely resembling this description appears in any other review I have seen of the show. You would think that Radiohead briefly transforming into Kiss circa 1975 would've been extremely newsworthy.)

Again, none of this really squares with what you hear on the recording of the show. It speaks to how much media narratives can shape how art is initially received. Perhaps British music scribes were expecting Radiohead to make their own version of a bleakly punishing Scott Walker album. Walker would eventually record himself pounding a slab of pork on one of his LPs. Upon its release, *Kid A*'s most virulent critics would accuse Radiohead of "pounding the meat" in the metaphorical sense.

The most famous tour that Radiohead did in conjunction with *Kid A* was the "tent" tour, a series of twenty-one shows in September and October played underneath a portable, 10,000-person capacity canvas structure free of any corporate branding. A literal rock-'n'-roll circus, the "tent" tour was inspired at least partly by *No Logo*, Canadian journalist Naomi Klein's bestselling anti–big business treatise that swiftly became a crucial text for the emerging anti-globalization movement in the early aughts.

Released in December of 1999, right as Radiohead was mired in the deepest, darkest frustrations of the *Kid A/Amnesiac* sessions, *No Logo* first became associated with the band via Ed's online diary. He name-checked the book twice in the spring of 2000, and the book eventually became a talking point in the band's profiles connected to *Kid A*. Three band members apparently read the book, and *No Logo* supposedly was even in the running as an album title for a brief time.

"*No Logo* gave one real hope," O'Brien later told *Q* magazine. "It certainly made me feel less alone. I must admit I'm deeply pessimistic about humanity, and she was writing everything that I was trying to make sense of in my head. It was very uplifting." Ed, always the resident hippie in Radiohead, even attended a demonstration against the World Trade Organization.

As for Thom Yorke, he apparently grew tired of Radiohead giving Naomi Klein so much free publicity. "He bats away our questions about *No Logo*," *Q* reported, "and shrugs that the book didn't teach him anything he didn't already know."

He might have also blanched at those who gave the book too much credit for influencing the lyrics of *Kid A*. Or maybe he was trying to distance *Kid A* from proclamations that it was some profound political statement about the new century. The whole point of pursuing his "cut-and-paste" lyrical style was to free Radiohead songs of the need to mean anything literal. You could read a song like "Idioteque" as a song about the evils of consumerism. ("Here I'm alive / everything all of the time.") Or you could *experience* it as the primal manifestation of a collective subconscious that just happened to come out of Thom Yorke's mouth when he was in a recording studio. I suspect he would prefer the latter.

This is not to say that *Kid A* is meaningless, or that one can't glean political or cultural meaning from it. It's just that this meaning would never be intrinsic. The extrinsic meaning of *Kid A*, in fact, wouldn't be apparent when it was released in October of 2000. It accrued, and evolved, over time, as the language of the album became less alienating and more intuitive.

The crux of *No Logo*'s argument is that it's the responsibility of each of us to carve out a space that is free of corporate control, money, and branding. For a band like Radiohead, which was very much ensconced in the highest echelons of the corporate music industry, that seemed all but impossible. But the "tent" tour was an attempt by Radiohead to control its own environment in the physical world, just as *Kid A* was Radiohead's bid to sequester itself from Muse, Travis, and all of the other bands that had taken up the mantle of majestic guitar-based rock in the style of *The Bends* and *OK Computer*.

Going it alone is easier said than done. Especially when you also have to be the focal point of the communion your fans share at concerts. For that reason, I find myself caring more about those seventeen shows Radiohead played before the "tent" tour, back in June and July of 2000, when they were playing many *Kid A/Amnesiac* songs for the first time. The run ended a week after that ambivalently received appearance at the Meltdown Festival, with three concerts in Israel. Though the climax was actually on July 4 in Berlin, when Radiohead played what many fans believe is one of their greatest shows ever.

The mood of that tour seems festive, like a much-needed holiday after being cooped up in various studios for so long. Ed, sadly, stopped updating his diary during this tour. His last entry was in Athens, Greece, on June 26. "A brilliant audience who exhibited great patience at hearing a set with nine new songs," he writes, "and a band which ignored repeated requests for 'Creep' (understandable on their part, the requests that is, as this was our first visit) and 'Pop Is Dead' (cheeky bastards)." ("Pop Is Dead," a non-album single from the *Pablo Honey* era, had been wisely cast aside from the band's live performances many lifetimes ago.)

O'Brien added that he was drinking "vast amounts of alcohol," like a proper rock 'n' roller, and that he was happy about how well "The National Anthem" and "Everything in Its Right Place" were going over. Though the woozy and knock-kneed "In Limbo" was still "a little tricky."

What's apparent when you listen to recordings of the earliest shows from June is that Radiohead, unsurprisingly, had to ease into the new material. Contrary to what some of the London-based music critics believed, Radiohead clearly did not want to turn off their fans. When the tour opened on June 13 in Arles, a small artistic community in the south of France, they played seven new songs, though "Optimistic"—which became the tour's usual opener—was slotted third after "Talk Show Host" and "Bones." Then came two other chestnuts, "Karma Police" and "Planet Telex."

They also played "Dollars & Cents," arguably the most challenging track they played live that summer, and possibly the inspiration for the "rehearsal-room jams" complaint in the aftermath of the Meltdown Festival. (I used to hate "Dollars & Cents" but it's now one of my favorites of this era. It sounds like Phish deconstructing one of Bernard Herrmann's old Hitchcock scores—and I swear that's a compliment.)

Tellingly, they didn't attempt "Dollars & Cents" again until June 25, in Thessaloniki, Greece. While "Dollars & Cents" eventually became a regular presence in setlists, they steered clear of the most potentially off-putting new tracks: "Hunting Bears," "Like Spinning Plates," and "Life in a Glasshouse" didn't make the setlist, while "Idioteque" and "Motion Picture Soundtrack" were saved for the fall.

If Radiohead's goal coming out of the endless experimentation of 1999's studio-bound hibernation truly was to kill every instinct they ever had about "big" rock music, their initial forays back into live performance must've seemed like utter failures. Because they still sound like the most awe-inspiring guitar band of their generation when you play those bootleg tapes. However, I don't really think killing the "rock" aspects of Radiohead's music was the goal. Maybe they *thought* that was the goal at some point. But on tour, they deliberately avoided playing the songs they knew would fundamentally alter the fabric of a Radiohead show. They knew, deep down, that you can't change who you are. And that, above anything else, is what comes through when you listen to bootlegs from the summer of 2000.

Radiohead's second concert in Berlin, on July 4, at a venue that held about 1,000 people, is the acknowledged high point of the tour. More than that, it's one of the all-time great Radiohead shows, in which the band was still drawing on the anxious energy of playing scores of new songs to a mostly unprepared audience. And yet, by this point in the tour, they also had an obvious confidence in their material and didn't feel as obligated to couch unfamiliar songs with reliable greatest hits.

Eleven out of the twenty-two songs played that night were new, including four out of the first five songs. The version of "In Limbo" is especially transcendent. And then there's the staggering take on "Kid A" that absolutely destroys the version on the album.

The studio take is a low-key hum, like a robot voice sending a distress signal from the deepest reaches of inner space. Live, however, Radiohead made "Kid A" sound like an excursion into *outer* space, a positively huge and demented sonic explosion punctuated with a wholly unexpected harmonica breakdown, like Bruce Springsteen discovering *Another Green World*.

Radiohead didn't play the spooky title track from their album all that much in 2000—it showed up six times on the summer tour, and not at all on the "tent" tour. The penultimate performance of "Kid A" that year was July 4. They had reached a peak and seemed to know it.

I saw a quote once—it must have been when I was in the midst of wasting several hours of my life on the Internet, and hating myself for it—that perfectly sums up the human condition for those of us who spend way too much time online: "The internet used to be a place where some people went to feel good about themselves. Now it's a place where everybody goes to feel bad."

Kid A now seems weirdly prescient about the latter statement. A tone poem about our "doomed-to-be-extremely-online" lives. But in the months leading up to the release of the album, it actually symbolized something entirely different. It made people feel *good* about going online. Kid A was a catalyst that provoked a subset of diehards to go on the Internet and commiserate about whether "Treefingers" was an ingenious homage to Brian Eno or the self-hating technophobe's version of a space-filling rap-album sketch. Put another way: in 2000, this one was kind of optimistic.

For Radiohead, Kid A was an attempt to sidestep the mainstream media. They wanted to escape the burden of "meaning," of signifying a specific idea that quickly becomes an albatross after being repeated 10,000 times, a fear ingrained from being a potential one-hit wonder. Here was a record that was as opaque as "Creep" was obvious. It was designed to find a discerning audience. Anyone who found it merely frustrating was not the sort of person worth engaging with anyway. In this way, the Internet would help Radiohead find the audience they wanted.

When Radiohead did give interviews, a recurring theme was their reticence to speak with mainstream music media outlets. "I think we're generally not very comfortable with the hype that surrounds the release of the record, that's one of the things that did our heads in with OK Computer," Ed explained to the website music365.com. In the same interview, Phil added, "That kind of limelight is a barrier for music as well. People aren't coming to it with an open mind. They've already had their opinions formed by it or are railing against those opinions."

The Internet, at that time, was *outside* the mainstream media, that loathsome monolith dominated by corporations and group-think. The online world was decentralized and fostered a plurality of voices. In 2000, *Kid A* didn't seem like a critique of that world. The album in a way *aspired* to it.

For many people, including myself, *Kid A* was the first major rock album that was experienced via the Internet. Fans went online to read Ed O'Brien's dispatches from the sessions. They could hang out on message boards to find out which songs were being played on the band's summer tour. They went on file-sharing services like Napster and LimeWire and downloaded concert bootlegs.

Eventually, *Kid A* itself leaked. Leaks soon became commonplace. But in 2000, possessing an album before it was released was, for most people, unheard of. It was like being handed a cheat code for life.

I try to remind myself of how awesome downloading music used to be. Because now it's about as thrilling as ordering paper towels from Amazon. The more convenient that downloading became, the less fun it was. In 2000, it could take an hour or two to download one song. And sometimes it wasn't even the song you really wanted, as MP3s were frequently mislabeled. (I'm convinced that some bands built entire careers this way. Countless fans were no doubt introduced to *Distorted Lullabies* by Ours or Muse's *Showbiz* while searching for Radiohead files. In some cases, you actually came to like the rip-offs.) Ultimately, you still had the theoretical ability to look up any song you wanted, for *free*, so who cared how long it took, or if you occasionally got the wrong free song?

This is probably the most exciting pop-culture period I'll ever witness firsthand. It's akin to what happened in Hollywood in the late '60s and early '70s, when the movie business swiftly moved from the "old" studio system to the "new" generation of Baby Boomers who ushered in a golden age of filmmaking informed by the aesthetics of European cinema and the idealism of insurgent hippie culture. In any documentary about this period, there is inevitably a clip of Clint Eastwood and Lee Marvin singing in the misbegotten 1969 musical *Paint Your Wagon*, a saggy symbol of the decrepit studio system, and then a smash-cut to Dennis Hopper and Peter Fonda riding motorcycles to the tune of Steppenwolf's "Born to Be Wild" in *Easy Rider*, also released in '69. It's the hackiest, and also the clearest and most instructive, way to depict the profound cultural shift of the time.

I love that period of cinema, but I was born right as it was coming to an end in the late seventies, just four months after the release of *Star Wars*. I was much older and far more lucid in the late '90s and early aughts, when an even more dramatic and far-reaching revolution occurred in the music business. Just like in Hollywood during the hippie takeover of the '60s, there were people who intuitively understood and accepted the changes being wrought by technology and changing generational attitudes, and those who pushed back. Lars Ulrich of Metallica, who became the unwitting poster boy for anti-Napster rock stars, was like *Paint Your Wagon*. And Radiohead was *Easy Rider*, at least as far as being associated with more progressive ideas about what the Internet could do for musicians and the music industry.

By mid-September, about two weeks before it was released, tracks from *Kid A* were available on P2P sites because Radiohead's record company, Capitol, had already put a stream of the record online. The label designed a music player called iBlip that streamed the entirety of *Kid A*, plus other content that could be updated, including the latest Radiohead news, recent live tracks, links to preorder the album, and enigmatic videos that lasted between ten and twenty seconds.

Then Capitol made the player available to anyone who wanted to post it. *Kid A* was the opposite of an online exclusive—the smallest music blog had the same access to the most anticipated rock album of the year as *Rolling Stone* or MTV. More than 1,000 different sites posted the *Kid A* iBlip, and the album was streamed more than 400,000 times before it was released in early October.

A major record label allowing the public to sample an album ahead of time—and essentially paving the way for that album to be pirated online—was truly a radical experiment in 2000. I found out exactly how radical when I met Robin Sloan Bechtel, who was Capitol's head of new media at the time.

Bechtel had already been working for the company in that capacity for seven years at the time of *Kid A*. Her progress at growing Capitol's online footprint had been frustratingly slow. Her grandest achievements up until then included developing a Beastie Boys screensaver and launching a website for the metal band Megadeth. She also helped Duran Duran become the label's first band to premiere a single on the Internet. But for the most part, few at the label cared about the web.

Bechtel helped to hatch the idea of streaming *Kid A* online several weeks before it was released. (She had personally heard the album under much more convoluted circumstances—Radiohead demanded that Capitol executives listen to the album on a bus driving from Hollywood to Malibu.) But it wasn't an easy sell.

"Everything in the industry at that point was like, 'The Internet isn't important. It's not selling records'—everything for them had to translate to a sale," Bechtel told me. "I knew the Internet was [generating sales], but I couldn't prove it because every record had MTV and radio with it."

Bechtel eventually convinced Capitol to put *Kid A* on the Internet three weeks before release, though in retrospect she suspected that the label didn't know "half the stuff we were doing." When the album already showed up on Napster by September 13, Bechtel didn't care—the streaming numbers allowed the label to track the listening habits of their customers.

It was a primitive form of the online-consumption data that companies would soon monetize in the years ahead. But for now, Capitol knew they had a hit on their hands.

One of those Radiohead fans who was illegally downloading *Kid A* that fall was a twenty-five-year-old rock critic living in Chicago named Brent DiCrescenzo.

"I remember sitting in my apartment at the time, at home, on a futon, with my laptop plugged in, and anxiously awaiting every download," DiCrescenzo told me when I interviewed him in 2015 for the website *Grantland*. He remembers waiting an eternity to download "Treefingers," and then realizing it was merely a brief interstitial track.

"It put so much importance on each individual track," he recalled. "Like, I just waited an hour for this one song and it's just an ambient song? Oh my God! This track is totally pointless!"

An Atlanta native, DiCrescenzo had moved to the Midwest in order to write for a relatively new and largely unknown indie-music website called *Pitchfork*. The site was founded in 1995 by a recent high school graduate from Minneapolis named Ryan Schreiber, who met DiCrescenzo on one of the music-geek message boards that they both frequented online in the mid-'90s.

Originally called *Turntable*, Schreiber soon changed the name to *Pitchfork*, after Tony Montana's tattoo in *Scarface*. Though the name would also signify the website's early, irreverent style, which relished any opportunity to rail against the excesses and general lameness of mainstream rock and pop music.

After relocating to Chicago in 1999, *Pitchfork* started to move in a slightly more professional direction. But the site's tastes and especially its style of writing remained proudly *anti*-professional. Like many *Pitchfork* writers at the time, DiCrescenzo despised the deferential, buddy-buddy, "color in the lines" style of rock writing that was practiced at major rock magazines.

"There really wasn't a great music outlet," he said. "In the early '90s, I found most of my music watching *120 Minutes*, reading *Alternative Press*, and reading *Spin*. All three of those things had become worthless at that point. Music magazines were going in a more pop direction." He then added, with a sardonic glimmer, "Of course, now *Pitchfork* writes about Taylor Swift, so I guess everybody goes that way."

As a writer, DiCrescenzo cared more about David Foster Wallace than Lester Bangs, whom he claims he hadn't even read at that point. DiCrescenzo, in fact, loathed rock criticism.

"I just hate the really preachy, pedantic kind of music writing, where it's trying to stroke its chin," he said. "I always wanted to put into writing the feeling that the album would give you. If it was a serious, emotional album, I'd try to be serious and emotional. If it was a goofy, half-thought, dumb album, I'd try to write something that was dumb and goofy."

From early on, one of the only mainstream rock bands that *Pitchfork* adored was Radiohead. Throughout its history, even as every other indie trend came and went and the site's sensibility leaned more and more toward mainstream pop, *Pitchfork* would continue publishing reverent-to-worshipful reviews of the band's records.

In 2000, few on staff loved Radiohead more than DiCrescenzo. He had seen them several times in concert at that point, often traveling long distances. In 1998, he road-tripped to Washington, DC, to see them at the Tibetan Freedom Concert. This was the year that a bolt of lightning struck a female fan while Herbie Hancock was onstage, causing her to go into cardiac arrest. (She was eventually resuscitated.)

That night, DiCrescenzo lucked into a secret show that Radiohead played in town at the 9:30 Club. They played "How to Disappear Completely" for the fourth time ever that night, after premiering the song just two months prior in Los Angeles. Brad Pitt and Jennifer Aniston, who took it all in from the balcony as a newly minted celebrity couple, were famously photographed at this show, looking extremely stoned. A peak '90s moment, and Brent was in the middle of it.

In the summer of 2000, DiCrescenzo traveled to Italy for one of the pre-release *Kid A* shows in Florence. There's a reference to that concert in the most famous piece that DiCrescenzo wrote for *Pitchfork*, the perfect-score 10.0 review of *Kid A*. It comes in the opening paragraph, though DiCrescenzo doesn't spell it out plainly. He doesn't spell out *anything* plainly in this passage:

> I had never even seen a shooting star before. 25 years of rotations, passes through comets' paths, and travel, and to my memory I had never witnessed burning debris scratch across the night sky. Radiohead were hunched over their instruments. Thom Yorke slowly beat on a grand piano, singing, eyes closed, into his microphone like he was trying to kiss around a big nose. Colin

Greenwood tapped patiently on a double bass, waiting for his cue. White pearls of arena light swam over their faces. A lazy disco light spilled artificial constellations inside the aluminum cove of the makeshift stage. The metal skeleton of the stage ate one end of Florence's Piazza Santa Croce, on the steps of the Santa Croce Cathedral. Michelangelo's bones and cobblestone laid beneath. I stared entranced, soaking in Radiohead's new material, chiseling each sound into the best functioning parts of my brain which would be the only sound system for the material for months.

If a single review can be credited with putting *Pitchfork*—the most important music publication of the early twenty-first century, and possibly the *last* important music publication—on the map, it was DiCrescenzo's review. Radiohead fans were eager to read any and all takes about the album as soon as possible, and *Pitchfork*'s review went up the day the album came out. In the days of treacherously slow print deadlines, same-day album reviews were still unusual in 2000.

But DiCrescenzo's review was also *different*, in the same way that *Kid A* was different. For those who went online because they wanted an alternative to the establishment music press, *Pitchfork* gave them something they couldn't read anyplace else.

The passage of time has made *Kid A* seem less polarizing. But DiCrescenzo's review of *Kid A* has not been diluted in the least. It doesn't seem like it's "only" from the year 2000. It's more like a review from the late '60s, during the druggy early days of rock writing. Or maybe it belongs in the year 2060—a strange, exotic time in which the English language has been chopped and screwed beyond all recognition.

Some of the language in the *Pitchfork* review of *Kid A* is evocative—the opening of "Everything in Its Right Place" is likened to "*Close Encounters* spaceships communicating with pipe organs," as "Thom Yorke's Cuisinarted voice struggles for its tongue."

Other lines, well, make no fucking sense whatsoever. "The butterscotch lamps along the walls of the tight city square bled upward into the cobalt sky, which seemed as strikingly artificial and perfect as a wizard's cap" is not the kind of prose that any reputable music magazine or website would publish today. And, for the most part, that's too bad.

What ultimately made *Pitchfork*'s review of *Kid A* required reading for any Radiohead fan in 2000 was its effusive, sky's-the-limit praise. "*Kid A* makes rock and roll childish," the site declared. "Considerations on its merits as 'rock' (i.e. its radio fodder potential, its guitar riffs, and its hooks) are pointless. Comparing this to other albums is like comparing an aquarium to blue construction paper. And not because it's jazz or fusion or ambient or electronic. Classifications don't come to mind once deep inside this expansive, hypnotic world . . . It's the sound of a band, and its leader, losing faith in themselves, destroying themselves, and subsequently rebuilding a perfect entity."

In time, *Kid A* would lose its ability to make twenty-five-year-old rock writers wax rhapsodic about its value as a game-changer. *Kid A* would no longer seem like a threat to the establishment; it would *be* the establishment. And *Pitchfork* similarly would move from the fringes to the very center of the publishing industry. Ryan Schreiber—who named his upstart music blog after a symbol for populist, outsider uprising—sold *Pitchfork* to the massive

New York publisher Condé Nast (known for titles such as *GQ*, *The New Yorker*, and *Vanity Fair*) for an undisclosed sum in 2015.

By then, the very idea of a music publication—*any* music publication—being a hub for a thriving counterculture had come to seem antiquated. It's not as if some other upstart media outlet has come along to replace *Pitchfork*, as *Pitchfork* had come along to displace *Rolling Stone* and *Spin* in the early aughts. The very idea of a relevant music publication had . . . disappeared completely. As DiCrescenzo, who left *Pitchfork* in 2006, put it, "The new *Pitchfork* is just people talking about stuff on Twitter."

Back in the year 2000, hearing a record for free before it came out, and then reading thousands of words written about it by people who were more like you than the typical rock critic, truly seemed revolutionary. It made you want to spend as much time as you could in the digital world, parsing songs by your favorite band with dozens upon dozens of strangers who had more in common with you than anybody in your "real" life.

Kid A didn't register as a warning about the dangers of the online world back then. It was an invitation to a place that seemed better than the one you were in. We argued with strangers for fun. We laughed until our heads came off. And we swallowed till we burst.

CHAPTER 5

WHINY OLD RUBBISH

In time, of course, *Kid A* would come to be regarded as a cultural landmark. At the end of the aughts, *Kid A* was named the best LP of the decade by *Rolling Stone* and *Pitchfork*. Was the fourth Radiohead record ever controversial? In terms of revisionist history . . . dissension over *Kid A* isn't happening.

"Nobody admits now they hated *Kid A* at the time, the same way folkies never admit they booed Dylan for going electric," rock critic Rob Sheffield once observed. "Nobody wants to be the clod who didn't get it."

But aside from Brent DiCrescenzo and his upstart *Pitchfork* peers, few in the press wanted to call *Kid A* a masterpiece in the fall of 2000. As Sheffield suggests, *Kid A* hate flowed freer than *Kid A* boosterism upon the album's release.

In the UK, the media response was especially withering. Radiohead had won over skeptical British music magazines with the messianic grandiosity of *The Bends* and *OK Computer*, albums that would come to define the sound of British guitar rock for the next few decades. But as often happens to bands who put out instant classics, the love that the British press had for Radiohead's early work was weaponized against their grand departure, *Kid A*.

The recurring complaint from British critics was that Radiohead had forsaken what they were good at (incredible guitar tones, operatic vocals, songs about totalitarianism that you can make out to) for *this*, whatever *this* was. At least two reviews used the same metaphor: Radiohead was now trapped inside of a proverbial bubble—cut off from the outside world, from human emotion, from the very things that had once made them great.

Select explicitly likened Thom Yorke to John Travolta in the 1976 TV movie *The Boy in the Plastic Bubble*, though the tone of the review was closer to *Battlefield Earth*. The magazine called *Kid A* "antiseptic," scoffing that the allusions to Aphex Twin, George Orwell's *Animal Farm*, and an impending apocalyptic ice age were overwrought and obvious. "Hardly loveable, it's nonetheless one of the year's most interesting records—a tripartite mix of puzzlement, irritation, and pleasure," *Select* concluded. "What's not present is as important as what's actually here. The main absentees, then, are choruses, coherent lyrics, crescendos and guitars: the very stuffing of *OK Computer*."

This was one of the more thoughtful responses from the British press. Most English critics wouldn't even concede that *Kid A* might be an interesting experiment. The overwhelming vibe was one of annoyance, a feeling of severe consternation that this band—which many UK critics hadn't wanted to like in the first place, back in the days of *Pablo Honey*—now had the nerve to put out a record that seemed designed to *make* them hate Radiohead. This wasn't music—it was a provocation, a finger-jab to the chest, an insolent "fuck-you!" move.

"For all its feats of brinkmanship, the patently magnificent construct called *Kid A* betrays a band playing one-handed just to prove they can, scared to commit itself emotionally," the *NME* alleged. "And isn't that what this is supposedly all about?"

If some UK music mags were merely bemused by *Kid A*, others reacted with scorn and even fury. "Well, I have to say that, upon first listen, *Kid A* is just awful," wrote *Mojo's* Jim Irvin, who proceeded to reiterate his "rehearsal-room jams" complaint from the Meltdown gig. "Too often it sounds like the fragments that they began the writing process with—a loop, a riff, a mumbled line of text, have been set in concrete and had other, lesser ideas piled on top."

And then there was Mark Beaumont of *Melody Maker,* who wrote the most infamous pan of *Kid A*, calling it "look-ma-I-can-suck-my-own-cock whiny old rubbish." It was the pinnacle of the impatience that British critics had with the album, and what it signified about Radiohead's unwillingness to just play ball already and show the boys in Travis how it's really done.

Above everything else Radiohead was suspected, oddly, of being insincere. *You can't be serious with this shit?* was the prevailing feeling. The greatest guitar-rock band in the world doesn't make an album like *Kid A* unless it's trying to prove something. *Right?*

In the United States the reviews were predictably kinder. Yes, it's true that Americans have a history of losing interest once their favorite British rock bands decide to turn down the guitar noise and make their "European" art records. But Radiohead was America's first. Jimi Hendrix had to leave and become a star in England before he was accepted as a superstar in his home country. But the inverse was true for Radiohead—in the States, they went from the poorhouse to the MTV Beach House in almost no time at all. Thom Yorke was never a creep in America. He always belonged here.

While American critics were just as confused by *Kid A* as their British counterparts, at least they were willing to give Radiohead the benefit of the doubt. *Billboard* was among the most enthusiastic outlets. "On its fourth album, Radiohead now stands alone at the forefront of experimental rock with *Kid A*, defiantly tearing up the blueprints of guitar-based music and reassembling them in awe-inspiring fashion . . . It is, without question, the first truly groundbreaking album of the 21st century."

Rolling Stone was more reserved but leaned in the direction of an endorsement. "*Kid A* is a work of deliberately inky, often irritating obsession," wrote David Fricke. "But this *is* pop, a music of ornery, glistening guile and honest ache, and it will feel good under your skin once you let it get there." *Spin*'s Simon Reynolds took a similar stance of qualified praise, admiring the album's daring while also noting, in a somewhat mocking tone, that Radiohead took itself way too seriously.

"There's always been something slightly uncool about Radiohead . . . Leaving hipster credibility to the Becks and Stereolabs, Radiohead lay their wares out in the stall marked IMPORTANCE," wrote Reynolds, who concluded with some prescient prognostication. "*Kid A* is not the career suicide or feat of self-indulgence it will be castigated as. The audience amassed through *The Bends* and *OK Computer* is not suddenly going to vaporize: Part of being into Radiohead is a willingness to take seriously the band taking itself *too* seriously."

The idea that Radiohead "takes itself too seriously" was already predominant in the conversation about the band during the OK *Computer* era, and had probably existed in some form from the moment that Yorke was heard singing "what the hell am I doing here?" on MTV. But it became permanently baked into Radiohead's persona with *Kid A*, the band's most overt "art rock" gesture.

In this way, the British and American press were united in depicting Radiohead as a band stuck in a kind of perpetual adolescence, forever obsessed with matters of personal identity and global instability. The implication is that the grown-ups writing about Radiohead were able to see these preoccupations for what they really were—kid stuff, silly and self-indulgent, the sort of dalliances you eventually move beyond with the benefit of perspective.

This was most famously expressed by *High Fidelity* author and occasional music critic Nick Hornby in a review for *The New Yorker*. *Kid A*, he wrote, "relies heavily on our passionate interest in every twist and turn of the band's career, no matter how trivial or pretentious. You have to work at albums like *Kid A*. You have to sit at home night after night and give yourself over to the paranoid millennial atmosphere as you try to decipher elliptical snatches of lyrics and puzzle out how the titles ('Treefingers,' 'The National Anthem,' and so on) might refer to the songs. In other words, you have to be 16."

In Hornby's view, *Kid A* was basically just self-important crap for teenagers, the very thing that "Creep" had once been accused of being. "The music critics who love *Kid A*, one suspects, love it because their job forces them to consume music as a 16-year-old would. Don't trust any of them," Hornby concluded. "I suspect that people who have been listening to rock music for decades will have exhausted the fund of trust they once might have had for 'challenging' albums. *Kid A* demands the patience of the devoted; both patience and devotion become scarcer commodities once you start picking up a paycheck."

I've always considered myself a Gen-Xer. But reading the reviews of *Kid A* reminds me that I'm actually a *young* Gen-Xer, and dangerously close to actually being a Millennial. Technically, I'm an Xennial, meaning I was born between 1977 and 1983 and share common characteristics with both generations.

For the most part, I think broad generational distinctions are dumb. Actual human beings can't be reduced to archetypes based on when they were born. That's not sociology, it's astrology. However, every now and then, there are generalities that can be accurately applied to certain demographics. This is one of those times.

I wasn't sixteen years old when *Kid A* came out. And I wasn't yet a professional music critic. Here's what I was: a twenty-three-year-old single guy who had been listening to Radiohead for more than 25 percent of his life. I was precisely the sort of person who listened to *Kid A* with *extreme* seriousness in 2000—and I did it without apology. I took it as a matter of fact that Radiohead was an important band, and that this was an important record. *Because it was important to me.*

Whether Radiohead took itself too seriously honestly never occurred to me. As far as I was concerned, they took themselves exactly as seriously as they should have. It's like accusing your car of taking itself too seriously for starting up once you put the key in. Actually, the car is just doing what it's supposed to do. And as far as I was concerned, Radiohead was supposed to make (yes) IMPORTANT albums like *Kid A*.

Like pretty much everybody else I knew, I was downloading music hand over fist. But I made a point of buying *Kid A*. I felt it *deserved* to be purchased. I wanted to play the CD while looking at Stanley Donwood's foreboding artwork, taking in those spiky whitecapped mountains as I peered into that bloody, dark-red horizon. Was this a sunrise or sunset? Was a fire raging behind those mountains, or were we seeing the last floating embers of an already extinguished flame? I pondered these questions with the utmost thoughtfulness.

When you took it home, the CD jewel case felt heavier than normal. Eventually, you realized there was a second booklet behind the plastic disc holder. (If the movie had existed at the time, this discovery would've made me feel like Nicolas Cage in *National Treasure*.) Inside the booklet, there was a series of run-on sentences about climate change and fascist governments and the perils of globalization.

"WATCH THE WORLD COLLAPSE LIKE A DISCON-TINUED COMPONENT IN A NEW OUTDATED AP-PLIANCE. YOU WILL SOON BE THROWN ON THE SCRAPHEAP WITH THE CORPSES AND THE FRIDGES AND THE CFCS + KILLERBEES." This was definitely the most subversive purchase I had ever made at a Best Buy.

It's hard to remember exactly how I heard *Kid A* in that moment, and what I thought about it immediately afterward. I don't think I had heard any of the songs beforehand. I had only read about them, and what I had read primed me to expect something potentially alienating and even unlistenable. But this actually made me want to like *Kid A* before I pressed Play, which will seem counterintuitive only if you didn't grow up listening to alternative rock in the '90s. The bands I came up on were expected to make the "difficult follow-up to the smash hit" album. After Nirvana's *In Utero*, Pearl Jam's *Vitalogy*, and Nine Inch Nails' *The Fragile*, I had been trained to expect a familiar arc—lots of poisonous pre-release buzz, followed by an album that was actually more accessible than the press had led you to believe.

That was more or less true of *Kid A*. I didn't love *Kid A* as much as *OK Computer*, because I didn't love *any* album as much as *OK Computer*. But I still really liked it, and I felt that way pretty much from the beginning. More than that, I *respected* it. I regarded Radiohead as my Beatles, and *Kid A* was their *Sgt. Pepper* move. *The Bends* had confounded me at first as a lover of *Pablo Honey*, and *OK Computer* briefly flummoxed me as an obsessive of *The Bends*. By the time of *Kid A*, I *wanted* Radiohead to fuck with me.

For weeks after I bought it, I listened to *Kid A* at least once per day. Even in the Wild West days of illegal downloading, you still didn't have access to *everything* like you do during the streaming era. So, you were more likely to sit with the same album for several weeks. Plus, I considered the albums I bought to be an investment. You weren't purchasing just a CD with your dollars, you were pledging a certain number of hours to that album to justify the financial setback. The accounting for time wasn't specific, it was a gut check you administered to yourself. Have I put $16.99 worth of time into this album yet?

As I pored over *Kid A*, I fell into a ritual. I would usually listen to "Everything in Its Right Place" at least twice in a row, or sometimes just the first ten or so seconds five consecutive times. That opening synthesizer was just endlessly spellbinding.

I almost always skipped "Kid A" for the first several months, and then I listened *only* to "Kid A" after it was used with great effectiveness over the closing credits of a *Sopranos* episode. "The

National Anthem" was an excellent track to play in the car, assuming I could get my janky Discman adapter to work. "How to Disappear Completely" was the choice headphone cut, especially after smoking a bowl.

Many times I would skip ahead directly to "Optimistic," because I was still deep down a basic *OK Computer* bro. But "Optimistic" was also the gateway to the superior second side of *Kid A*. It was here that the constant criticisms about the album "not having any songs" completely fell apart. "Idioteque" wasn't a song? "Morning Bell" wasn't a song? *Were these people even listening?*

Kid A took on a different meaning one month later, when the Bush versus Gore presidential election came and refused to go. I would put Radiohead on headphones sometimes as I stayed up all night, night after night, and watched the news reports. In time, as some votes were counted and many more were discounted, the suggestion that an album referencing *Animal Farm* in the year 2000 was somehow beyond the pale instantly seemed like a relic of a more privileged time.

When critics claim that a band takes themselves too seriously, what they're really saying is *we're too old* to take seriously this thing that the generation behind us loves. Now that I am one of those music critics, I try to remember this whenever I write about a band like Twenty One Pilots, the Ohio-based arena-rock act that seems ridiculous to me but is profound to millions of teenagers. Talk to any of those fans, and they'll tell you about the dense web of mythology that links each song on every Twenty One Pilots album, and how this is ultimately manifested in the onstage personas in the two (not twenty-one) core members of the band.

Frankly, it's not something that I care about. But I appreciate how much it matters to *them*. They don't take that band too seriously. They care about them just as much as I cared about

Radiohead in 2000. It's good to at least entertain the possibility that *not* having the time to invest in art means that you're *less* qualified to comment on it. You are, at best, a tourist in a land that you will never be able to inhabit or even fully comprehend.

The reason Radiohead fans were passing around the *Pitchfork* review of *Kid A* was because it spoke to us on *our* level. (It was also hilarious, for not wholly intentional reasons.) *Pitchfork* didn't qualify its praise or concede any of the criticisms made by the band's detractors. The review was written by a guy young enough to believe that Radiohead had earned our devotion and therefore justified all of the time and headaches required to make, and then appreciate, *Kid A*. All of the mainstream critics were our big brothers and sisters, the people who thought they knew better but would forever be on the outside.

The Hornby review got passed around too—more as a rumor than anything else, a dispatch from the land of the clueless fuddy-duddies. You almost felt sorry for these people: how sad must it have been to not marvel at the exhilarating weirdness of seeing Radiohead perform on *Saturday Night Live* less than two weeks after *Kid A* was released?

Kate Hudson was the host that night. This was during her initial rush of stardom from *Almost Famous,* an epic about the twentieth-century rock mythology that *Kid A* had sought to put in the cultural rearview. Radiohead had been playing the new songs on the road then for about four months, and any early butterflies about how the material would go over were long gone.

Rather than play "Optimistic" or "How to Disappear Completely" or even "Morning Bell," Radiohead went right for the thorniest bits from *Kid A*. First up was "The National Anthem," complete with a screeching seven-piece horn section that sounded like a ska band dying a slow, painful death inside of a trash compactor. While Ed worked his Infinite Sustain guitar and Jonny plucked away on his ondes Martenot, Thom whipped his head in front of the mic for a full sixty seconds before singing a word. Later, when he started to dance during the climactic horn-section bloodbath, he flailed like a man being consumed from head-to-toe by bees.

But the performance that everybody remembers came next, when Radiohead played "Idioteque." And what people remember the most is Jonny Greenwood playing a modular synthesizer, manipulating the cables to control the beats, though everyone thought he was actually directing long-distance calls on the East Coast in the year 1961.

Here was Radiohead doing what their critics said they shouldn't do—not playing guitars, not playing beautiful melodies, not at all resembling a conventional rock band. Was this really happening?

"This is really happening," Thom implored.

In the final sixty seconds, the song fizzled into full-on delirium. The beats accelerated. Feedback washed over everything. Thom was still fighting invisible bees but for a moment he seemed to be winning. It sounded like nothing but freeform noise, and utterly unlike anything that had ever blared out from Studio 8H, or any other network show.

If you got *Kid A*, it felt like the future—*your* future—had arrived.

A common complaint about *Kid A* for those who had seen Radiohead on the summer tour or heard the bootlegs was that many of the most Radiohead-like songs didn't make the album.

For instance, during those early shows, "Pyramid Song" had been the most reliable showstopper, at least judging by the concert reviews and the enthusiastic responses that can be detected on bootlegs. The song was a cousin to "Everything in Its Right Place"; Yorke wrote it the same week, though he ultimately decided that it sounded better unadorned by the electronic fuckery that submerged "Everything."

Fans originally referred to it as "Egyptian Song," after it was performed publicly for the first time in June of 1999 at the second Tibetan Freedom Concert. The debut was stark and a little shaky, with Yorke playing alone at a piano to a quiet and fitfully interested audience, evoking John Lennon stripping himself back to the extremes of *Plastic Ono Band*. When Radiohead recorded "Pyramid Song," it benefitted greatly from Phil Selway's sensitive, swinging drumming, which recalled one of the song's inspirations: Charles Mingus's "Freedom," from *The Complete Town Hall Concert*.

Two other regulars from the summer tour, "Knives Out" and "You and Whose Army?," were also missing in action from *Kid A*. While neither song straight up replicates the sound of *The Bends* and *OK Computer*, you could place them on the same continuum as those albums much easier than "The National Anthem" or "Idioteque." They are, essentially, pretty pop-rock songs with hummable melodies and easily discernible choruses.

Thom Yorke loathed at least one of those tracks. "For the longest time I really, really hated that song," he said of "Knives Out" in a 2001 *Mojo* interview. "Knives Out" was already infamous for supposedly taking 313 hours to record, which Yorke said was the case "'cos I hated it so much."

For those who viewed *Kid A* as a willful negation of Radiohead's strengths, the knowledge that Radiohead had classic-sounding material on the back burner undoubtedly added to the feelings of frustration. Almost immediately, there was anticipation in some quarters—mainly the British press—for the *next* Radiohead album, which would include the songs left off of *Kid A* and, presumably, restore their status as a guitar-slinging arena-rock band.

That album, *Amnesiac*, came out just eight months later, on June 5, 2001. In England, *Amnesiac* was greeted as a corrective to its predecessor, sometimes in blunt, downright disrespectful terms. ("Relax: It's Nothing Like *Kid A*" the *Guardian* promised.) In America, however, *Amnesiac* was praised but also treated as something of an afterthought. At least two publications, *Spin* and *Entertainment Weekly,* dubbed it "Kid B." *Rolling Stone* conceded in an otherwise positive reviewed that the album can "inevitably, be heard as leftovers from *Kid A*." Even *Pitchfork* gave it *only* a 9.0, a significant step down from the evangelism of the *Kid A* review.

As for me, I was bored with *Amnesiac*. In time, I would come to appreciate it as a lesser but nevertheless still pretty great extension of *Kid A*, the rare sequel that seems disappointing at first but gradually seems better and better each time you watch it. (It is *The Fast and the Furious: Tokyo Drift* of Radiohead albums.) But in 2001, it seemed like the worst of both possible worlds for Radiohead—not a full-fledged return to '90s guitar-rock splendor, nor a meaningful extension of the breakthroughs made with electronic and improvisational music forms on *Kid A*. It felt like both a retreat and an echo, a reminder of what Radiohead had just accomplished and a failure to either extend or transcend it.

Amnesiac is structured as the inverse of *Kid A*, which starts out weird and dark and disjointed and turns warmer and prettier and more welcoming on side two. In contrast, *Amnesiac* is ridiculously frontloaded. Radiohead seemed to be saying, "Oh, you want 'Pyramid Song' and 'You and Whose Army?' do you? Fine, take them off our hands. Now we can get back to the weird shit we really care about." Along the way there is another skronky free-jazz song, "Life in a Glasshouse," and another version of "Morning Bell." Neither is as good as its companion track on *Kid A*.

Whereas *Kid A* works as a seamless mood piece, flowing from one song to the next with an unusual but unerring sense of interior logic, *Amnesiac* is all over the place. For years, I would drop out of *Amnesiac* after "Knives Out," the midpoint and the unofficial conclusion of the "anti-*Kid A* appeasement" portion of the album. But now I find myself gravitating more to side two, which starts with the nightmarish redux of "Morning Bell/Amnesiac," and then slips into the simmering malevolence of "Dollars & Cents." By the time the album wraps with the migraine-inducing whirring of "Like Spinning Plates," *Amnesiac* feels more like two EPs—one commercial, one experimental—that have been packaged together than a cohesive whole.

My biggest problem with *Amnesiac* is contextual. Radiohead knew they had more great songs than they could fit on *Kid A*. And they suspected that some of those songs might not work as well if they put them on the same record. They were also wary of putting out a double album—that bloated, old-world, classic-rock vehicle for conveying A Serious Artistic Statement, the sort of well-worn trope they were trying to escape. Right or wrong, Thom Yorke didn't have any Billy Corgan–style megalomania in him, no matter his ample supply of mellon collie or his ability to conjure infinite sadness.

But putting out another album so similar to *Kid A*, their big break with their own past, was inevitably going to sandbag the sequel. No matter how good the songs were on *Amnesiac*, the boldness of *Kid A* was going to make those *Amnesiac* tracks sound worse. It's hard to declare that you're setting a course for the future when your next move is an album that pleasantly evokes what you've just done.

Again, once both albums were removed from their moment, the contradictions and tensions of *Kid A* and *Amnesiac's* imperfect marriage would make them even more interesting. But the polarizing, love-it-or-hate-it immediacy of *Kid A* could only diminish the relatively safe *Amnesiac* in its wake.

A question that every Radiohead fan asks at some point is "Should *Kid A* and *Amnesiac* have come out as a single album?" A super LP that includes all of the best songs from both records— what would that look like, exactly?

Most of the time, the question goes unanswered. What right do we have to question our heroes? If they felt that the mountain of music they created through 1999 and early 2000 had to be released on *Kid A* and *Amnesiac*, then it was clearly the correct decision.

But let's say, *purely for the sake of conversation*, that you are an A&R executive working for Parlophone in the spring of 2000. One day, Thom and Jonny walk into your office with a stack of tapes. *We've had it*, they say. *We can't figure out what in the hell to put on the next record.* (Perhaps they would say "bleedin' record," because they're British and this might be one of those stereotypes that proves to be true.) At any rate, they *need* you to help them turn this music into a brilliant, digestible fourteen-track record.

I'm not one to leave Thom and Jonny in the lurch. Therefore, I have made my own version of *Kid Amnesiac*. And I have to say: I think I A&Red the hell out of this. It's not only the best Radiohead album, I think this would have been the best album of the aughts. Which is a pretty big deal, given that *Kid A* is already the best album of the aughts—at the very least, I don't think that I made the album worse.

KID AMNESIAC **TRACK LIST**

Side A
1. "Everything in Its Right Place"

No question this was going to make it. It's impossible to separate this song from this period in Radiohead's career. Yorke warbling "Yesterday I woke up sucking a lemon" over a sinister keyboard lick unquestionably defines the sound of this era. More than that, the conception, writing, and recording of this song is kind of *the* point of *Kid A*. However, the inclusion of "Everything in Its Right Place" means that *Amnesiac*'s very good but similar opener, "Packt Like Sardines in a Crushd Tin Box," has to go. If "Packt" were to make the album, it would have to go side 1, track 1, because it serves the same tone-setting role. (To make a Roxy Music analogy, Bryan Ferry is "Everything in Its Right Place," and Brian Eno is "Packt Like Sardines in a Crushd Tin Box"—two charismatic frontmen who ultimately can't coexist in the same band.) Instead, it will have to live in an alternate universe with "beloved B-side that many fans insist should've made the album" status.

2. "The National Anthem"

There's room for only one free-jazz odyssey on my album, and I must go with the propulsive, rock 'n' roll one over "Life in a Glasshouse," the "draggy, kinda dull New Orleans jazz funeral" one. "Life in a Glasshouse" is one of my least favorite songs on either *Kid A* or *Amnesiac*. I don't hate it, exactly—being one of the lesser songs on those albums only means you've fallen short of a very high bar. I just think that "Glasshouse" verges a bit on "experimental rock" self-parody. In a retrospective piece for *Rolling Stone*, Rob Sheffield called the horn section on "The National Anthem" a "cornier-than-usual art-rock cliché," adding that the "'bad horn section as symbol of alienation' thing had been done a time or two before." But I think that criticism actually applies better to "Life in a Glasshouse," which is just one overly craggy vocal away from being a full-on Tom Waits homage.

3. "Pyramid Song"

After two defining *Kid A* mindfuckers, a sharp turn toward the majestic. Putting "Pyramid Song" in the third slot immediately alters the character of this mythical fourth Radiohead record. *Kid A* was purposely constructed to sound dim, monochromatic, and claustrophobic, creating a sensation that feels like being handcuffed to a bed in a darkened room. Once you put "Pyramid Song" in the mix, however, you have opened a window. The first two tracks here are all dread and foreboding; now, suddenly, there's nothing to fear, nothing to doubt.

There's something almost Zeppelin-esque about it. That's partly due to the title: "Pyramid Song" slots neatly between "Immigrant Song" and "The Rain Song" on a playlist of tracks with self-evident fucking grandeur. I also detect a flash of "Kashmir"—Thom Yorke jumps in the river where there's no denyin' that Robert Plant has been flyin' in similar waters, given that they both wound up encountering a moon full of stars and astral cars.

4. "How to Disappear Completely"

In the context of *Kid A*, "How to Disappear Completely" is the "normal-sounding acoustic ballad" track. But in the context of this imaginary record—which is a bit more dynamic and less centered on suffocating techno-horror—the oddness of the arrangement is teased out more. You focus less on Thom's voice and guitar and more on the disoriented swirls of the orchestra that are slowly erasing him.

5. "Dollars & Cents"

In 2009, *Spin* ran a takedown piece based on the tiresome premise that Radiohead is universally adored by critics, and therefore must be denounced as the boring and pretentious band that it *really* is. (Never mind that the very existence of a takedown piece instantly discredits the notion that "everybody" loves Radiohead.) At the core of the article is an argument that Radiohead is secretly a jam band, a designation that is automatically construed as an insult even if it's never explained *why* it is insulting.

Even when the writer attempts to describe a recent Radiohead concert as tedious, he can't help but make Radiohead sound amazing: "They kept going, one groovy tone poem into another, masterfully weaving beats, sound-washes, and misty vocals into an immersive experience of sound, light, pattern, rhythm, and utter, paralyzing boredom." Somehow, only the "utter, paralyzing boredom" part feels incongruous and just plain wrong.

The fact is that Radiohead did flirt with aspects of jam-band-dom during the *Kid A/Amnesiac* era, most notably in "Dollars & Cents." Though the model wasn't the Grateful Dead, but the German rock band Can. Holger Czukay, Can's bassist and cofounder, directed the band to jam in the studio, after which he would piece together the improvised music into songs. Radiohead attempted the same on "Dollars & Cents," recording eleven minutes of noodling that Yorke later called "incredibly boring." But then they chopped out about six minutes, added some strings arranged by Jonny that Thom felt were needed "to give it a sort of authority," and this wobbly, unsettling song was born.

6. "Optimistic"

7. "In Limbo"

I couldn't bear to split up the best pairing on *Kid A*. One is a straight arrow who plays by the rules. The other is a loopy rule-breaker of questionable sanity. What links them is a funky jam that sounds like the Isley Brothers sitting in with the Mos Eisley cantina band from *Star Wars*. I did move them together from the start of *Kid A*'s second side to the end of this album's first side. Coming after "Dollars & Cents," this feels like the appropriate conclusion to the "jammy" part of *Kid Amnesiac*.

SIDE B
1. "Cuttooth"

My favorite B-side from this era, with all due respect paid to "Worrywort" and "Fog." On this album, it goes from B-side to the top slot on side B. With its rollicking piano and barreling groove that keeps on chugging along for more than five minutes, "Cuttooth" always seemed a little too epic to be relegated to extra-track status on the "Knives Out" single. (It's like U2 deciding that "Where the Streets Have No Name" would've been better suited as a B-side to "When Love Comes to Town.")

It supposedly came close to making *Amnesiac*, showing up on a promotional copy that was serviced early to French radio. In his diary, Ed O'Brien writes about "Cuttooth" several times, describing it as "the song with little structure" where "the only certainty is a bass riff." He likens the song credibly to yet another German band from the '70s, Neu!, whose records uncannily replicate the sensation of flowing water traveling downstream.

2. "Knives Out"

In the spring of 2000, when the British press was speculating on what the next Radiohead album would sound like, there were reports that Jonny Greenwood was obsessed with *Hatful of Hollow*, the 1984 compilation of B-sides and BBC radio sessions by the most important British rock band of the 1980s, the Smiths. "Knives Out" was the only song to subsequently come out of the *Kid A/Amnesiac* sessions to even vaguely support this assertion. Though I don't think it sounds *that* much like the Smiths—the only *Hatful of Hollow* track that's comparable is "Please, Please, Please, Let Me Get What I Want," though "Knives Out" doesn't plead so much as seethe menacingly, in the style of Yorke's old favorite, Elvis Costello. "If you'd been a dog / They would have drowned you at birth" sure makes those pleasingly jangly guitars seem a lot less sweet.

3. "Morning Bell"

This has always been a dark-horse favorite on *Kid A*. It's not the *greatest* track or the *most adventurous* or *the one that best exemplifies this era*. It's simply one of the songs that I most want to hear, every single time I put on *Kid A*, because I never tire of it. It's the best fusing of Radiohead's classic '90s "mid-tempo ballad" sound with the "forward-thinking" sensibility of the 1999–2000 sessions. It's like "Karma Police" after a *Bitches Brew* phase.

In the studio, the band had to beg Jonny Greenwood to play guitar on "Morning Bell," Yorke later claimed, because Jonny was preoccupied with putting his damn ondes Martenot on everything. Forcing Jonny to play guitar against his will has typically produced genius Radiohead moments going all the way back to "Creep." In "Morning Bell," there is no melodramatic *kachunk*; Jonny instead slowly releases his surliness like toxic fumes seeping out of a balloon, weaving tarantula-like lines in the song's smoldering final moments.

4. "I Might Be Wrong"

Yorke claims that he wrote and recorded this song after seeing a ghost in his house. "I live on a beach and one night I went out on my own and looked back at the house and even though I knew there was nobody there, I could see a figure walking about inside," he told *Mojo*. "Then I went back to the house and recorded that track with this presence still there."

It sounds like the sort of story that became associated with David Bowie during his mid-'70s L.A. period, when he was snorting enough cocaine to keep all five members of Fleetwood Mac standing upright and having all kinds of dark hallucinations. But the only thing messing Yorke up was his ambivalence about his own success.

"When someone's constantly trying to help you out and you're trying to express something really awful, you're desperately trying to sort yourself out and you can't—you just can't," he said. "And then one day you finally hear them—you finally understand, after months and months of utter fucking torment: that's what that song is about."

5. "You and Whose Army?"

The obligatory "political" song. The spooky echo effect on the vocal—which was intended to evoke the Ink Spots, a popular vocal group from the 1930s and '40s who predated doo-wop—was created in part by something called the Palm Speaker. It makes "You and Whose Army?" sound like a prewar blues record, as future generations will come to understand prewar blues in the year 2900, when all humans are living on Mars.

When Radiohead first started playing "You and Whose Army?" in the summer of 2000, Yorke would pointedly dedicate it to Tony Blair. By the end of the tour cycle in 2001—at which point the world had been turned upside down by September 11— he was directing the song to George W. Bush. What started as a snarky tweak had turned into a fearful, and trenchant, prayer against self-inflicted mass destruction. That's one hell of a journey for a song to take during the course of one tour.

6. "Idioteque"

Purists will protest about separating this song from "Morning Bell," as that transition is nearly as perfect as "Optimistic" melting into "In Limbo." But my instinct is to put "Idioteque" in the penultimate slot. It is part of the trio of most essential tracks from this period, along with the prominently situated "Everything in Its Right Place" and "The National Anthem."

7. "Like Spinning Plates"

Just as *Kid Amnesiac* can have only one undeniable opener, it can have only one inarguable closer. It was either this or "Motion Picture Soundtrack," and I'm going with the one that reminds me of experiencing a low-level tinnitus hum after hours of screamingly loud music. (But in a good way.)

"I think 'Spinning Plates' is the best of all the record for me," Yorke claimed. "When I listen to it in my car, it makes the doors shake." There's also something fitting about ending this album with a track that is based on a backward recording of "I Will," which eventually appeared on the next Radiohead record, *Hail to the Thief*. They probably nicked that idea from *Revolution in the Head*, Ian MacDonald's book breaking down the recording of every Beatles song, which Yorke was reading during the sessions.

In their own way, Radiohead took twentieth-century rock music, flipped it over, turned it into a heady blur, and then charged forward.

CHAPTER 6

ROBOT BOYS

Tom Cruise woke up sucking a lemon.

I remember thinking this as I sat in a theater watching Cameron Crowe's *Vanilla Sky* for the first time. I used to believe this occurred in the late fall of 2003, during the film's opening weekend. But I was wrong about that.

Here's what I know to be true: *Vanilla Sky* opens with one of the most famous movie stars of all time waking up to "Everything in Its Right Place." Tom Cruise is sprawled facedown on a bed in what appears to be an extremely nice Manhattan apartment. (It's located inside of the Dakota, the iconic building where Mia Farrow was hounded by imaginary Satanists in *Rosemary's Baby* in 1968, and where John Lennon was murdered by a real-life fan in 1980.) We see Tom get up, turn off his television (it's playing Billy

Wilder's *Sabrina*), pluck a gray hair out of his skull, put on a shirt, and head out into the world.

The whole scenario would seem mundane if it weren't for the sound of Thom Yorke's voice and that worrisome keyboard riff. The song tells us that something is about to go wrong. If it weren't for the presence of *Kid A*'s first track, this could almost pass for a scene from *Jerry Maguire*. But the song immediately puts you in an anxious frame of mind. In the audience, there are two colors in our heads. And one of them is black.

Out on the street, Cruise is in his car and driving to work. He looks around and notices that he is alone—nobody else is driving, nobody else is walking, there are no signs of life anywhere. He looks at his watch. It's 9:05 A.M. Thom sings that everything is in its right place but this is obviously an ironic commentary on the situation. *Nothing* is in its right place.

Soon, the song fades out as Tom pulls into an empty Times Square. He gets out of his car. He runs. Of course he runs—he's Tom Cruise, the most prolific runner in cinematic history. We can no longer hear Radiohead except in our own heads. The assumption is that either Tom is dreaming, or he's dead. A few moments later, we see him wake up back at the Dakota. But you still suspect that he might actually be dead.

I thought back to *Vanilla Sky* as I prepared to write this book, and I immediately remembered it as one of the first mainstream American films to comment on the September 11 terrorist attacks. And I was curious about how *Kid A* fit with that. Initially, my unreliable memory constructed a narrative in which I recognized this right away upon my first viewing. Tom Cruise plays a rich, handsome, and self-involved heir to a media empire who selfishly uses women as playthings for casual sex, and then carelessly throws them away. But when Tom tries to pull this with an unstable acquaintance played by Cameron Diaz, his life takes a tragic turn. He winds up horribly disfigured after a car accident, which robs him of his confidence and prompts him to question the very foundations of his life and sanity.

According to my memory, I watched *Vanilla Sky* in 2003 and viewed Tom Cruise's character as a metaphor for America, and Cameron Diaz as a foxy stand-in for Al Qaeda. It seemed like such an obvious interpretation. After all, the hijackers crashed United Airlines Flight 175 into the south tower of the World Trade Center at 9:03 A.M., just two minutes before Tom Cruise looks at his watch in the opening of *Vanilla Sky*. And Crowe used *Kid A*—an album that has come to be associated with the paranoia and fear that descended on the world after 9/11—as the soundtrack. This couldn't have been a coincidence. In fact, Cameron Crowe was laying it all on pretty thick.

But it all really *was* a coincidence. *Vanilla Sky* didn't come out in 2003, it was actually released two years earlier, on December 14, 2001. The Times Square scene was filmed on November 12, 2000—about five weeks after *Kid A* was released, and ten months *before* 9/11. In one scene, you can actually see the World Trade Center, a shot that Crowe insisted on keeping in the film in spite of protests from the producers of *Vanilla Sky*.

As for Radiohead, Crowe says on the DVD commentary track that he played *Kid A* a lot on the set, mostly at the insistence of Jason Lee, who was a big fan. (Crowe's tastes seem more rooted in the L.A. rock of the 1970s, and contemporary artists who draw on that tradition. I'm guessing his favorite Radiohead song is "High & Dry," because it sounds a bit like "Peaceful Easy Feeling" played about twice as fast.)

Given that *Kid A* was a new album at the time, it makes sense that it would be an "of the moment" record during the production of *Vanilla Sky*. (Crowe also makes Tom Cruise a Radiohead fan in the movie, having him reach for a CD, presumably *Kid A*, during an early scene in which he's driving to work with Lee riding shotgun. I would bet that Tom definitely loves "Paranoid Android," because as a Scientologist he is surrounded by paranoid androids.)

My mind had retconned *Vanilla Sky* as a 2003 film because it *seems* like it has the perspective of a movie made two years after September 11, in much the same way that *Kid A* was subsequently recontextualized as an album about (or at least linked with) September 11. For Crowe, *Vanilla Sky* (which is a remake of a 1997 film, *Abre Los Ojos*, by Spanish director Alejandro Amenábar) was the *Kid A* of his filmography, his grand attempt to take his established formula—witty and occasionally saccharine romantic comedies—and subvert it with surrealism, philosophy, and purely visual storytelling that risked leaving the audience feeling confused and even alienated.

In this analogy, *Jerry Maguire* is *The Bends* (the purest example of his early style, and a blueprint that many others ripped off) and *Almost Famous* is *OK Computer* (the epic that distills his entire career up until that point, acting as an effective endpoint for his "early" period). With *Vanilla Sky*, he was trying to go deeper, darker, and stranger. In the process, like Radiohead, he would deconstruct the very archetypes that he had helped to create and popularize in the culture.

The existential dread that pervades *Vanilla Sky*, and *Kid A*, would come to be viewed by future generations as manifestations of that post-9/11 period when there was a genuine belief that irony (and maybe even mass entertainment in general) were no longer tenable as an antidote to the horrors of the real world. The overriding theme of *Vanilla Sky* (as well as *The Matrix, Mulholland Drive, Donnie Darko, Being John Malkovich,* and other films released around the turn of the century that deal explicitly with the so-called "nature of reality") is that people delude themselves about who they really are, and that in order to know "the truth" you have to completely upend (or even destroy) your life. For Radiohead, and to some degree Cameron Crowe, this process also involved taking apart the most grandiose and commercial excesses of their own art, in order to get at something more difficult and "real."

Watching *Vanilla Sky* now is an odd experience—though not necessarily in the same way that the movie seemed odd when it first came out, when many viewers and critics merely found it pretentious and bewildering. (Cameron Crowe and Radiohead both faced hostile treatment from the press for their bold, "experimental" provocations.) Now *Vanilla Sky* just seems weird by how weirdly prescient it is, as a film about twenty-first-century America that had no intention of being a film about twenty-first-century America.

The film's original ending is particularly disturbing—Cruise is on top of an extremely tall building, and he must hurl himself off the roof in order to "free" himself from the lucid-dream state into which he has willingly put himself. This imagery unwittingly evoked the famous "Falling Man" photo, taken by Richard Drew, of an anonymous person choosing to end his life on his own terms, right before one of the WTC towers collapsed. Coming so soon after 9/11, the ending of *Vanilla Sky* shook audiences already sensitive to the horrors being beamed out to them every night that fall on television from Ground Zero. "When Tom jumps off that building, you could feel the wave go over the audience," Crowe later recalled in an interview with the website Film School Rejects. "People were electrified, whether positive or negative."

Kid A would similarly be credited with "predictive" powers in relation to 9/11 in a passage from Chuck Klosterman's 2005 book, *Killing Yourself to Live.* Klosterman writes about how "Everything in Its Right Place" evokes the city waking up, just as Crowe associated it with Tom Cruise crawling out of bed. "Kid A" is the sound of people going to work, and then "The National Anthem" signifies the mania of the attack. "How to Disappear Completely" is about the feeling of numbness that first greeted the attacks. His analysis goes from there. (I'm guessing that anyone who chose to read a book about *Kid A* is probably familiar with this essay. It has since either been quoted or appropriated on at least five thousand different Reddit pages.)

When you read the book, however, it's clear that Klosterman doesn't believe that Radiohead *literally* foresaw Osama bin Laden planning a terrorist attack on the United States. ("I am not saying that we should have been warned by it, or that John Ashcroft should have played *Kid A* in spring 2001 and said, 'You know, we really need to ramp up airport security,'" he writes.) He just notes the strange ways in which the album seems to align with the events of that day, just as *Vanilla Sky* happened to accidentally harmonize with the single most haunting photograph associated with September 11.

The obvious flaw in the "*Kid A* predicted 9/11" theory is that the album is too lyrically opaque to point to *anything* remotely concrete, much less the worst tragedy in American history. The era's other fluky 9/11 album, Wilco's *Yankee Hotel Foxtrot,* coincidentally hits it on the nose with far greater precision, with songs like "Jesus, Etc." that reference how "tall buildings shake / voices escape singing sad, sad songs." (Though, like *Kid A*, *Yankee Hotel Foxtrot* was recorded before September 11.)

In reality, *Kid A* (as well as *OK Computer* and maybe even *Yankee Hotel Foxtrot* and *Vanilla Sky*) were actually informed by the residual anxiety left over from Y2K, the turn-of-the-century would-be disaster that was supposed to be the technological equivalent of 9/11 and has since been totally forgotten. The specifics of Y2K are now so arcane that it's virtually impossible to convey how scary it was to contemplate in the late '90s. Essentially, the idea was that computers would malfunction once their internal calendars flipped to 2000, because they wouldn't be able to distinguish the new year from the year 1900, causing the collapse of vital systems around the globe.

Most people didn't take Y2K seriously enough to join a survivalist militia and hole up in the woods with lunatic gun nuts. But everyone I knew was at least *slightly* freaked out by it. My girlfriend at the time and I actually drove around all night and waited out the New Year on a lonely country road, just in case society suddenly descended into riots. (I was otherwise unprepared for the possibility of this event. If forced to hunt and gather for food in a post-Y2K wasteland, the only tool at my disposal in the car was a CD copy of Built to Spill's *Keep It Like a Secret*.)

But even when Y2K didn't bring about the end of the world, it did leave you with these unshakable feelings of both vulnerability (because it showed just how much technology controlled our lives) and oppression (because it showed just how much technology controlled our lives). And this made you want to believe that, maybe, there was still a world beyond this matrix of dependence and imprisonment, a tough but pure "reality" concealed by the comfortable but curdled "dream" of modern life.

Getting to that place was of paramount importance, even if it required throwing yourself (or just your guitars) off the top of a tall building.

On September 11, 2001, Radiohead did not perform as visionary oracles. Instead, they acted like a normal professional rock band under extraordinary circumstances.

Radiohead was back in Berlin on 9/11, for their first concert in the city since the triumphant pair of gigs fourteen months earlier, before the release of *Kid A*. This time, Radiohead was nearing the end of the tour cycle for *Amnesiac*. After Berlin, there was just one more stop on the European tour in Ireland, and then a short run of shows in late September and early October in Japan.

The terrorist attacks in New York City occurred just hours before that night's concert. It doesn't appear that Radiohead ever seriously considered canceling, as many bands who had shows booked on September 11 did that day.

A window into the band's frayed state of mind comes courtesy of an interview with Ed and Phil conducted right after that concert, and presumably aired on German television weeks later. (An apparently unedited video of the interview lives on, via YouTube.) The guys are understandably shell-shocked and awkward. The interviewer asks if he can include questions about the day's events, though the main thrust of his inquiry includes the usual stuff about why *Kid A* and *Amnesiac* don't have the sorts of "real songs" that other Radiohead albums have. (At one point the reporter mentions that he had just interviewed Scott Weiland of Stone Temple Pilots, who loved Radiohead but didn't get *Kid A*.)

"In no way was it a mark of disrespect," Phil says about the band's decision to perform. "We would have let down a lot of people tonight . . . We generally felt numb today. What can you say that doesn't sound trite?"

This same "what can you say?" tension pervades the actual show. Listening to the bootleg, the gig initially unfolds like pretty much any normal Radiohead show from the era. The band plays well but unexceptionally—which means they were actually playing with superhuman focus and skill, given the circumstances. Holding it together enough to pull off a mediocre Radiohead gig in the immediate aftermath of September 11 has to rank among the band's most difficult feats of mental and physical strength.

In the early going, it's tempting to discern nods to the tragedy that probably aren't there. Opening with the unruly violence of "The National Anthem" seems significant . . . until you notice that Radiohead opened every single concert from 2001 with that song, save for a performance recorded for French television in April. Yorke doesn't actually acknowledge what's happened until about forty minutes into the concert, before they play "Airbag."

"I'm trying not to say anything," he says with an exhausted edge in his voice. He might be responding to a heckler in the audience. "Well, what the fuck are you going to say after today, you know? There's absolutely nothing *to* say."

Then, near the end of the main set, he decides to address it head-on. "So who here doesn't know about it? Everybody knows what I'm talking about? You don't know about the airplanes in America?" Yorke asks. The audience sounds restless—they're either reluctant to confront the horror or unsure about what Thom's getting at. This is a rock singer stopping a rock show to make a painful middle-of-the-night phone call.

"Somebody tell them," he says. Then, he realizes there is no other "somebody." You can feel him sigh. "I'll tell you," he surrenders.

He doesn't know all of the facts. He isn't sure how many planes have crashed, or whether any of them were actually shot out of the sky. What he suspects is that the world has changed forever, and now he's trying to process it in real time. "That's why, you know, things are a little mute tonight," he says. "I'm sorry about that. This is called 'Paranoid Android.'"

From there, the show takes a decisive turn. Rock concerts are typically described as avenues for collective catharsis, where people can leave their troubles behind and experience community with strangers who have temporarily abandoned their own traumas. But there is no such release apparent when you listen to this concert. What you detect instead is a burgeoning, ineffable feeling of doom—not just for what might happen on September 12, but for what might happen in the years and decades that lie ahead in the twenty-first century.

Yorke proceeds to dedicate two songs to the Bush administration during the encores: the confrontational "You and Whose Army?" and the resigned, mournful "Street Spirit." "This is hoping . . . George W Bush doesn't declare World War III," he says before "Street Spirit."

While *Kid A* wasn't the act of an oracle, that dedication certainly was.

When Ed O'Brien and Phil Selway sat down for that German TV interview on September 11, 2001, they didn't just fumble for the right words in the aftermath of unspeakable tragedy. They were also asked to give a sound bite about the Strokes.

"A good debut record," Ed offered weakly. "Tight band."

While *Kid A* was remembered after the fact as an album that foreshadowed the gloom of the post-9/11 world, in the immediate aftermath of the tragedy no band dominated the music press like the Strokes. In the moment, an album like *Kid A* that hit the nose on collective dread so directly was simply intolerable. Of all the stages of grief, the first is denial, and that was manifested by the first Strokes record, *Is This It*.

Here was a band that reinstated everything that *Kid A* had seemingly sought to dismantle: guitars, leather jackets, curly hair and perfect cheekbones, clanking beer bottles, cocaine afterparties, machismo, all that classic-rock hero bullshit. Their sense of timing was incredible: *Is This It* was supposed to come out in the United States just two weeks after September 11, 2001. Then it was delayed for a few more weeks, just in time for people to start feeling grateful again that they were still alive. Now we wanted to make the most of it. And where better than in New York City, our nation's most fantastic metropolis, a stand-in for old American ideas about reinvention and boundless possibility that we all still wanted to believe in and *Is This It* personified.

I was a Radiohead fan who had bought into *Kid A*, but it didn't take long for me to switch allegiance to the Strokes. I was already a goner by the end of the video for "Last Nite." It was a brilliant commercial for the Strokes experience, as powerful as "Paradise City" was for selling Guns N' Roses, or "Even Flow" was for Pearl Jam. What "Last Nite" communicated was that the Strokes were a five-headed gang. They weren't the last great American rock band, but they were the last rock band in which each member had a clearly defined personality.

Anyone could see that there was a clear hierarchy in place, with Julian Casablancas and Albert Hammond Jr. installed as the unquestioned Mick and Keith commandos out front. (Or, if you prefer: the Thom and Jonny.) But the other guys were also crucial to the operation. Nick Valensi was the "rock 'n' roll Stroke," which was easy to spot due to his resemblance to Izzy Stradlin. Nikolai Fraiture was the "stoic Stroke," which put him on the same continuum as Bill Wyman of the Rolling Stones and John Entwistle of the Who. And Fabrizio "Fab" Moretti was obviously the "Ringo Stroke," due to his cute nickname, endearingly low-key demeanor, and the fact that he coincidentally played the drums.

In the "Last Nite" video, the camera slowly pans from left to right as the Strokes play on a stage that's been outfitted to look like a TV variety show from the '60s. The imagery instantly evokes the archival clips we've all seen of the Beatles and the Stones performing on Ed Sullivan or *The T.A.M.I. Show*. The hype here was not subtle, but it also didn't seem unwarranted. Like those old bands, the Strokes looked amazing. (The most Strokes-like quote ever, given by Albert Hammond to *Spin* in 2003: "Since I was 15, I've had a motto that you should always look like you're onstage.") Better yet, they were *familiar*. The first time you saw them, you felt like you had already loved them for ten years. For a populace afraid that everything that had once seemed indestructible was now on the verge of collapse, this sort of reassurance felt necessary.

Practically from the moment that the Strokes were first written about, they were cast in a narrative about the "return of rock." The media wanted them to be the new Nirvana, the underground underdog who comes from out of nowhere and transforms the culture, ushering in a wave of like-minded bands that clean out the dregs of mainstream rock. Radiohead had been one of the bands who followed in the wake of Nirvana once upon a time.

Rock 'n' roll legend credited Nirvana with ending hair metal ten years earlier, and now music critics hoped that the Strokes would do the same to the absurdly popular likes of Korn, Limp Bizkit, and Creed. Though savvier critics were quick to call the White Stripes the true Nirvana heir, recasting the Strokes as the Pearl Jam of the "return of rock" movement. (In this scenario Interpol is Alice in Chains, the Yeah Yeah Yeahs are Soundgarden, and Kings of Leon are Radiohead. Don't blame me, blame this flawed "grunge to early aughts indie" conversion chart.)

But Nirvana didn't actually kill off hair metal—Mötley Crüe and Poison stayed on the road for decades after *Nevermind*. They wrote bestselling memoirs and starred in medium-popular reality shows, and even had their songs turned into a Broadway musical, *Rock of Ages*. Those bands were durable, like road cases and leather pants. It was the grunge bands, save Pearl Jam, that couldn't survive the '90s.

But old myths die hard. With the Strokes, people really wanted to believe that they could (and did!) change the world. And that continued even after the Strokes proceeded to fall apart in the wake of *Is This It*. I remember reading a tenth-anniversary retrospective piece about *Is This It* in which the writer claimed that the Strokes "kicked the nu-metal blight to the curb." This somehow became conventional wisdom as the "return of rock" era itself became the subject of romantic nostalgia. But what were we *actually* missing?

The Strokes represented the last gasp of dominant mainstream twentieth-century music press, the leviathan that *Pitchfork* and other Internet outlets were in the process of usurping. The music industry itself was imploding, descending into a decade-plus valley that wouldn't turn around until the advent of streaming platforms. In *Meet Me in the Bathroom*, Lizzy Goodman's compulsively readable oral history of NYC rock during this period, she uses music blogger Sarah Lewitinn's tale of two very different listening parties as a metaphor for the industry collapse.

"When *Kid A* came out in 2000, a bunch of us were invited to the Hudson Hotel to listen to the album on sick speakers and it was catered," Lewitinn said. "By 2004, when [Interpol's second album] *Antics* was coming out we found ourselves in a hotel room with Ritz crackers, beer, and a tiny little tinny-sounding boom box. That's how far the industry had fallen."

But there was no better metaphor for this period than the Strokes themselves. They became very famous in 2001, which was maybe the last year when if you became very famous, you pretty much stayed famous forever. And then they proceeded to get fucked up on booze, drugs, and megalomania.

In the 2010s, the Strokes were relegated to a side project for Casablancas's main musical focus, his bonkers prog-slash-vaporwave-slash-cock-rock band the Voidz. But they still had enough celebrity power to headline music festivals. Onstage, they projected the old mystique; in fact, it was easier now, since there was no baggage about them being rich, privileged trust-fund kids. Getting older meant they were no longer pretty, which made them even better Strokes, as projecting mystique was what they were always best at.

But while the Strokes achieved eternal fame, they weren't actually *popular*. As it is with so many critics' darlings, what made the Strokes an obsession for the press proved to be a liability commercially. The Strokes were a band for people in their twenties. They sounded best played loud in a bar at closing time. They were referencing things that Gen-Xers thought were cool—Lou Reed, CBGB, acting glamorous and lazy simultaneously.

But *popular* rock bands have always been for teenagers. They have to articulate a point of view that speaks to teens universally ("life sucks") and also addresses youth culture at this specific moment ("life sucks because technology/the environment/ capitalism/my complexion has progressed in an especially dire direction"). The Strokes never had that one defining anthem that would have made them matter to Millennials. Their "Smells Like Teen Spirit." Their "Creep." Their "One Step Closer."

How could the Strokes (or *Kid A*) kick nu metal to the curb when the curb was *owned* by Linkin Park in the aughts? No rock band sold more records during that decade. It took about two years for *Is This It* to move as many units as Linkin Park's second proper album, 2003's *Meteora*, sold in its *first week*. The band's most successful LP, the 2000 debut *Hybrid Theory*, eventually moved 20 million copies. And you can bet that nearly all of those CDs were bought by kids who either couldn't figure out how to download *Hybrid Theory* illegally, or really wanted a good-sounding physical copy that they could blast the shit out of in their cars.

Hybrid Theory came out near the end of October of 2000, just three weeks after *Kid A*. "One Step Closer" had already been out for a month. For a while, Linkin Park's sales lagged behind Radiohead's, with *Hybrid Theory* moving just 50,000 records in its first week, or about a quarter of what *Kid A* did in its first week. But then *Hybrid Theory* went gold relatively quickly, right as the holiday shopping season was kicking into high gear. In 2001, it exploded, selling 4.8 million copies, making it the year's bestselling record. The year after that, *Hybrid Theory* was still selling 100,000 copies per week at times.

Upon the release of *Kid A*, Thom Yorke declared that "alternative rock needs bludgeoning to death on a big stick and left on a bridge to warn passers-by." But this was just rhetoric. *Kid A* was still a rock album, and it was part of a classic continuum that included the Beatles, David Bowie, Talking Heads, and U2. The very idea that rock needed "bludgeoning to death" was part of the melodramatic life-death-rebirth cycle that's at the very heart of rock mythology, whether it's punk, grunge, or the "return to rock" bands of the early '00s. The desire to demolish the paradigm was part and parcel of the belief that the paradigm still mattered.

Linkin Park meanwhile wasn't part of that continuum, and while *Hybrid Theory* wasn't presented as a revolutionary game-changer, it ultimately had a more profound impact on rock music than *Kid A*. What Radiohead had struggled for more than a year in the studio to conceptualize in their own minds—how do we stop being a grandiose guitar-rock band whose music derives from our influences in the '60s, '70s, and '80s?—was never an issue for Linkin Park, because they were already part of a world in which that kind of trad-rock was a nonentity. It's like the difference between studying for years to learn French, and being born and raised in France. Linkin Park *parlaient la langue de la* youth culture like Radiohead hadn't since *Pablo Honey*.

Radiohead approached the twenty-first century by emulating old heroes like Brian Eno and David Byrne. But that wasn't really the music of the future. In the new century, popular rock bands survived by melting into hip-hop and pop music, assembling their records the way a DJ or a superstar producer would, as a collagist assembling and disassembling infinite layers of sonic information. For Linkin Park, this resulted in a form of music that couldn't be described strictly as rock or hip-hop, but rather as a *hybrid* that spoke to an audience that increasingly saw genre distinctions as irrelevant.

Like Radiohead, Linkin Park came from an undistinguished background. Formed in 1996, they were originally known as Xero and they spent years trying to get their act together as a rap-rock band. It wasn't until they found singer Chester Bennington that the Linkin Park sound began to take shape. Like Julian Casablancas, Bennington was fashion-model handsome, though his look was less "rock dude" than "slightly edgy boy-band member." He resembled Justin Timberlake after smoking a single cigarette. But he was also a gifted singer in a scene where conventional singing was largely viewed as passé. The contrast between Bennington's uplifting vocals and co-frontman Mike Shinoda's rapping would exist at the heart of Linkin Park's biggest hits for the next several years.

Their first hit was "One Step Closer," a song about all of the usual teenage problems—nobody understands me, nobody will listen to me, nobody takes me seriously when I say *THATI'MABOUTTOBREAK!!!* In the video, Bennington's short, bleach-blond locks and weirdly angelic glow in spite of the performative angst are vaguely reminiscent of Thom Yorke in the "Creep" video. He's straining to let you know that he doesn't belong here, while Shinoda plays the screeching, disruptive Jonny Greenwood role with his percussive holler.

Linkin Park also had some of Radiohead's wholesomeness. No matter the puffed-up fury of their delivery, the guys took pride in not relying on the sort of wanton vulgarity associated with the biggest nu-metal bands of the '90s in order to sell records. As

Bennington told *Rolling Stone*, they "didn't want to make a big point of not cussing," but they also resisted hiding "behind anything to show how tough we can be."

In the same *Rolling Stone* profile, Bennington and Shinoda also make a point to present themselves as clean-living, decadence-free rock stars. "If one of us wants to drink or smoke, we do it in the club, not in the bus, so people who don't want to drink or smoke can hang out in the bus," Shinoda says. Later, Bennington adds, "If you're getting wasted, you should be spending that energy out there meeting your fans. I love to get compliments from the janitors in the clubs—'Dude, thanks for not destroying the place, I can go home early tonight.'"

Just as Radiohead built a career in the early '90s with a backbreaking tour schedule, Linkin Park became the biggest band of the early twenty-first century by playing 170 shows in 2001 alone. And after the show, they would step out into the audience to shake hands, give bro hugs, and sign autographs. In the studio, they were just as hardworking—during the recording of *Meteora*, they wrote forty different choruses for "Somewhere I Belong," a process even more tedious than the fabled 313 hours Radiohead spent on "Knives Out." Though in Linkin Park's case, the perfectionism was in service of making a huge hit—"Somewhere I Belong" eventually became Linkin Park's second number-one alternative song.

As Radiohead tried to run away from rock radio with *Kid A*, Linkin Park started building an empire based on an ability to craft hugely successful songs that never seemed to leave the airwaves. Between 2001 and 2010, they had ten number-one alternative hits, and an additional five songs that made the top ten. They also had three top-ten hits on the pop charts, culminating with the biggest song from *Hybrid Theory*, "In the End," which peaked at number 2.

In retrospect, Linkin Park's rise had none of the "return to rock" pretensions that defined the Strokes epoch. As the decade unfolded, Linkin Park's music soundtracked the gradual extinction of rock radio itself. By the mid-aughts, rock stations were already disappearing from major markets like Chicago, Seattle, Philadelphia, and Baltimore. Some of this was due to changing listener habits that caused ratings for alternative stations to crater by as much as 20 percent in some markets in the crucial eighteen-to-thirty-four demographic. But another pivotal change had to do with the fragmentation of rock's audience, and how the differing constituencies had become completely incompatible. To put it somewhat reductively, there were Linkin Park fans, who wanted nothing to do with Internet-native indie rock, and Radiohead fans, who rolled their eyes at bands like Linkin Park. You couldn't appeal to one without estranging the other. So, rock stations in many places simply disappeared.

In the end, the idea of an album like *Kid A* destroying old-world rock music was a nonstarter, because the infinitely more popular *Hybrid Theory* had waged a friendly coup with a more radio-friendly formula that ultimately de-emphasized guitars and traditional rock tropes. But even Linkin Park eventually wanted to rebel against the machine by making their own *Kid A*.

Just as Radiohead pulled their radical left turn on their fourth album, Linkin Park made their fourth proper LP, 2010's *A Thousand Suns*, a stylistic shift into arty electronica. A concept record about nuclear-assisted Armageddon, it indicated that fears about the state of mankind were not strictly a turn-of-the-century concern. Linkin Park had just capped off the most commercially successful decade for any rock band in the aughts—now they wanted to make an album that quoted Martin Luther King and '60s student activist Mario Savio's "Bodies Upon the Gears" speech, while also downshifting musically into trippy, vibed-out soundscapes. "Fuck it, we're just going to go bonkers," Bennington promised.

My favorite track on A Thousand Suns is "Robot Boy," because it could almost pass for a parody of Kid A. (Bennington was on record as a Radiohead fan.) There's an arch piano lick, a skittering electronic beat, a droning string section, and conspicuously treated vocals. Though Linkin Park, of course, is more direct about delivering a clearly stated message: "Hold on, the weight of the world / will give you the strength to go."

In the end, Linkin Park fans hated A Thousand Suns. While the band reverted back to its familiar sound on subsequent albums, A Thousand Suns signaled the beginning of their commercial decline in the 2010s, which came to a sad end when Bennington took his own life in 2017.

For Radiohead, finding a way to survive in the aftermath of deconstructing their music would prove nearly as difficult.

PART THREE
AFTER KID A

Help me get where I belong . . .

CHAPTER 7

WE'VE GOT HEADS ON STICKS

s *Kid A* political? My heart says yes but my brain is . . . confused.

When I hear "Idioteque," I sometimes think it's about the climate crisis, even though Thom Yorke is an unreliable weatherman. (I *wish* an ice age were coming.) Still, "let me hear both sides" distills the crisis of our contemporary discourse perfectly—climate denialism serves no purpose when "this is really happening." A few songs earlier, "Optimistic" sums up how self-destructive self-interest enabled by capitalism is destroying the planet: "The big fish eat the little ones / Not my problem, give me some."

All of this *seems* obvious when I listen to *Kid A*. But I also know that none of it is *actually* happening. Thom Yorke purposely compiled his lyrics in random order, picked out the lines that sounded cool but were otherwise nonsensical, and distorted his voice to the point where most of what he was saying was unintelligible anyway. And yet listeners still strained to interpret *Kid A*'s "message," because all of the subterfuge that Yorke insisted on putting between himself and his audience only made the album seem that much more mysterious and profound, like a religious code that only true believers can decipher.

As one of those meddlesome close listeners, I'm also skeptical about how my reading of *Kid A* happens to line up with what I already believe. *Am I thinking way too much about this? Is it possible that there really isn't anything there?* Only a critic who is lying to himself doesn't worry about this sort of thing.

I felt personally and professionally implicated the first time I watched Rodney Ascher's fascinating 2012 documentary *Room 237*. The movie features five people who have obsessively watched Stanley Kubrick's 1980 horror masterpiece, *The Shining*, dozens, if not hundreds, of times. In the process they've all come away with incredibly complex and positively batshit interpretations of what the film "actually" means.

Of course, I'm not the first person to think about Stanley Kubrick while also contemplating Radiohead. Around the time of *OK Computer*, it became standard for music critics to compare the ornate and sleek contours of Nigel Godrich's sci-fi production style to a dazzling and discomforting Kubrickian Steadicam shot. They evince a similar hopeless coldness toward humankind, from a perspective that resides slightly outside the mainstream while also managing to be extremely commercial. But really, Radiohead and Kubrick belong together because they both invite intense (over)analysis to the point of unhealthy obsession, often among bearded, middle-aged nerds (like me).

Room 237 presents this sort of overthinking at its most riveting and disturbing extreme. One guy is convinced *The Shining* is about the Holocaust. Another guy postulates that it's about the genocide of Native Americans. My favorite theory is that *The Shining* is Kubrick's confession of guilt over helping the US government fake video footage of the Apollo 11 mission. To support these arguments, the analysts go deep into the subtext of the movie, pointing out the secret significance of Danny's (Apollo 11!) sweater, Jack's (German!) typewriter, the Calumet Baking Powder cans stacked in the hotel's pantry ("Calumet" means "peace pipe"!), and the phantom hard-ons of the Overlook Hotel's manager (because they're just creepy). One person even insists that Kubrick put his own face in the clouds that hover behind his name in the opening credits. Why? *Because it's a secret message.*

It's all very interesting, while never seeming the least bit credible. Frankly, everybody in *Room 237* comes off as an incredibly smart and impressively articulate lunatic. However, one of the interviewees does make a trenchant point about the nature of audiences—it ultimately doesn't matter what the artist intended. Meanings can exist whether the creator consciously put them there or not. Sometimes, an artist can put things into their work without realizing it. Or the audience might hear or see things that aren't "supposed" to be there, but are made real because "we" put them there.

In this context, even a lack of "meaning" is meaningful. *Kid A* unfolds exactly as the Internet does. It is obscure and inexplicable and moves relentlessly forward without bothering to explain itself, offering no context outside of our own personal biases, opinions, and limited consciousness. And yet . . . we understand it intuitively. We've all become postmodern interpreters of the world, gleaning meaning from the accidental juxtapositions of disconnected data that come across our social media feeds.

Things no longer have to make sense for us to make sense of them. We can make our own realities. They report, we decide. In a way, listening to this album so much in 2000 prepared millions of brains for how to perceive "normal" reality as it would come to be defined in the twenty-first century. It's why *Kid A* sounds like classic rock now.

Radiohead fans clearly have put a lot into *Kid A* that the band didn't necessarily intend. If you study the text of the record, it doesn't seem political at all. This changes somewhat if you read the liner notes tucked into the jewel case of the CD, or consider Ed O'Brien's endorsement of *No Logo* and Thom Yorke's support of the Jubilee initiative to forgive Third World debt, both of which coincided with the making of *Kid A*. Though it's still not an ideological album. There are no slogans on *Kid A*, only non sequiturs.

And yet it *feels* political, and that *feeling* informs how the songs are perceived. Listening to *Kid A* replicates the sensation of living in the twenty-first century and being deeply enmeshed in technology and cut off from the most primal aspects of human existence. Though it doesn't tell you what to *do* about this, as political music usually does. *Kid A* merely puts you in a headspace to experience your own dissatisfaction in a heightened sonic environment. It's the difference between going to the hospital and looking up your symptoms on WebMD. Listening to *Kid A*, you feel intense anxiety without the promise of a cure, the very heart of the human condition at a time of infinite information and nonexistent solutions.

Ultimately, there's not much you can point to that "proves" *Kid A* has any perspective on the world as it stood at the turn of the century. There is no single "statement" lyric that you can turn into a standalone meme. It's not like Public Enemy's 1989 classic, "Fight the Power," the greatest protest song of my lifetime, which directly spells out a critique of contemporary society. When Chuck D says, "Our freedom of speech is freedom or death / we've got to fight the powers that be," he leaves no room for doubt as to what he's talking about. Nobody listens to "Fight the Power" and thinks, *The subtext of this song is about how Public Enemy felt in the summer of '89 that Jack Nicholson's performance in* Batman *was a touch too broad.* There is no point in "interpreting" this song. You know immediately what "fight" means, and what "the power" is, and how Chuck D feels about it. "Fight the Power" makes itself clear in exactly four minutes and forty-two seconds. Meanwhile you can listen to *Kid A* for twenty years without ever getting to the bottom of it.

That's not the sort of directness with which Thom Yorke operated in 2000. Deep down he was still that college kid from Exeter who felt ashamed when a friend told him his lyrics were too obvious. And he was the rock star who for years had to live down the rank melodrama and plainly stated, radio-friendly angst of "Creep." If he ever had the capacity to write a song as obvious as "Fight the Power," it had long since been bred out of him by the media and his own self-consciousness.

It's as if being earnestly political in a song was almost embarrassing to him. Sucking a lemon was more dignified by comparison.

If Thom Yorke had been more of a polemicist, he might have stated his themes more directly. Instead of "big fish eat the little ones," he could have said, "We are consumers. We're the by-products of a lifestyle obsession. The things you own end up owning you." Instead of sonically twisting the most pointed lyric on *Kid A*—"We've got heads on sticks / you've got ventriloquists," from the title track—beyond the point of comprehension, he could have just said, "You're not the car you drive, you're not the contents of your wallet." Rather than title the album after a mythical clone of a human being, Radiohead might have just called it *Tyler Durden.*

Why am I linking *Kid A* to *Fight Club*, the most controversial film of the late '90s, and a problematic favorite decades later due to a vocal fanbase that includes incels, white supremacists, and various other undesirables who took exactly the wrong message from the film? Am I going down my own *Room 237* wormhole?

Not exactly. But also *not* not exactly.

One of the most interesting thought experiments to play with *Kid A* is to imagine how the album's subtext would have changed had Thom Yorke become involved in the production of *Fight Club*. Because in actual fact, the stars of the movie, Brad Pitt and Edward Norton, really did personally reach out to Yorke sometime after the *OK Computer* tour, sending over a copy of the script and asking if he would compose the score.

Pitt and Norton were fixated on *OK Computer* during the film's grueling 129-day shoot. (When Pitt was spotted with Jennifer Aniston at that 9:30 Club show in June of 1998, the one when Radiohead played "How to Disappear Completely" for just the fourth time ever, he was just starting to make *Fight Club*.) Norton said later that the two actors listened to Radiohead on repeat while on set. On the final night of filming, they stayed up until 4 A.M. playing *OK Computer* over and over.

Based on the 1996 novel by Chuck Palahniuk, *Fight Club* was envisioned by director David Fincher as a subversive anticonsumerist manifesto presented in the guise of a big-budget studio picture. He also saw it as a comedy, in which a delusional narrator (Norton) goes from grousing about the emptiness of Starbucks and khakis to plotting terrorist schemes with his charismatic friend Tyler (Pitt), who just so happens to exist only in his head.

For Fincher, the antiestablishment terrorism and fascist politics of *Fight Club* were never meant to be taken literally, even if he also strongly related to the Norton character's disillusionment with encroaching corporate totalitarianism. "We were making a satire," Fincher maintained later. "We were saying, 'This is as serious about blowing up buildings as *The Graduate* is about fucking your mom's friend.'"

You can hear echoes of Radiohead during one of *Fight Club*'s most famous satirical sequences, when the living room of Norton's bland apartment is digitally outfitted to look like the inside of an IKEA catalogue.

"If I saw something clever like a little coffee table in the shape of a yin-yang, I had to have it," Norton drones. "The Klipske personal office unit, the Hovetrekke home exer-bike, or the Johannshamn sofa with the Strinne green stripe pattern. Even the Rizlampa wire lamps of environmentally friendly unbleached paper. I'd flip through catalogs and wonder: What kind of dining set defines me as a person? I had it all."

What the scene most immediately evokes is "Fitter Happier," *OK Computer*'s most direct (and least interesting) song about how corporate culture socially programs all of us to associate "happy" lives with consumption and participation in capitalism. The way that "Fitter Happier" communicates this is not subtle—a robot voice mechanically advises against drinking too much and advocates for "exercise at the gym, three days a week" and "getting on better with your associate employee contemporaries," among other soullessly expressed platitudes.

You could also imagine this scene being set to "Everything in Its Right Place," as the song title plainly states the thematic point of the scene. Either way, Norton sounds like a guy lost inside of a Radiohead song. A zombie haunted by insomnia because his job requires him to travel constantly, he doesn't know where the hell he's going at a thousand feet per second. A true paranoid android.

In the end, Yorke begged off because he was a little too much like the guy in *Fight Club*. Yorke was burned out from the road, and (as we all know) he was about to enter a period of prolonged writer's block that would eventually culminate in the creation of two new Radiohead albums. "I went 'Nah, I can't.' I couldn't," Yorke said later. "I wouldn't have been able to do it then, but every time I see the film I go 'Oh . . .'"

Norton claimed, in a 2019 interview with journalist Brian Raftery, that Thom Yorke told him that Radiohead had *Fight Club* "on in the bus all of the time" during the *OK Computer* tour. Of course, this would've been impossible, as Radiohead was deep into the making of *Kid A* and *Amnesiac* when *Fight Club* was released in theaters in the United States in October of 1999, and in the UK the following month. What's more likely (assuming the part about Radiohead binging on *Fight Club* is true) is that Radiohead watched it during the *Kid A* tour, which opened the same month that *Fight Club* came out on DVD, and subsequently sold 6 million copies on the way to becoming a massive cult hit.

The implication from Norton is that *Fight Club* influenced Radiohead. While the timeline doesn't really fit, the movie (as well as Palahniuk's book) do come from similar sources of inspiration as *Kid A*. They're all end-of-the-century imaginings of the apocalypse, in which the end of the modern world is both something to be feared as a cataclysmic death, and embraced as an invitation for a spiritual rebirth, as a new life beyond the soul-destroying remnants of omnipresent corporate culture. (This idea is taken to another level in the movie version, when Norton's unnamed narrator, with the help of his alter ego, Tyler, brings down a series of high-rise buildings representing the infrastructure of the credit-card industry, another act of eerie 9/11 artistic foreshadowing.)

The roots of *Kid A* and the *Fight Club* movie intersect in 1998, the year when Y2K hysteria was starting to peak, inspiring the most fervent survivalists to start stockpiling food, 500-gallon tanks, and AR-15 assault rifles. One of the year's bestselling books was *Time Bomb 2000*, a guidebook for surviving the disaster that sold more than 150,000 copies in '98, before being translated into Japanese, Spanish, and Portuguese.

You can still buy the book online. It's like a time capsule from a cursed alternate universe. "Essential reading for everyone who wants to survive Y2K!" the marketing materials promise. "This edition contains updated coverage of every major aspect of society, including communications, power distribution, transportation, finance, travel, medicine, social services, education and employment."

Maybe we missed out when contemporary society wasn't completely remade at the beginning of the twenty-first century. *Fight Club* and *Kid A* are fantasies of what might have been. When Norton says, "Every evening I died, and every morning I was born again, resurrected," it points toward, "Here I'm alive, everything all of the time," from "Idioteque," as well as Yorke's messianic insistence on publicly killing Radiohead's past during the making of *Kid A*, so they, too, could be reborn.

Upon its release, *Fight Club* underperformed at the box office, and was excoriated by film critics. Roger Ebert, who actually liked *Fight Club* more than many of his peers, still called it "the most frankly and cheerfully fascist big-star movie since *Death Wish*," a work of "macho porn . . . in which eroticism between the sexes is replaced by all-guy locker-room fights." Even in Hollywood, *Fight Club* was despised. A story in the *Hollywood Reporter* polled anonymous industry insiders who decried *Fight Club* as "absolutely indefensible" and "deplorable on every level." The head of the studio that made *Fight Club*, 20th Century Fox, was fired the following year by Rupert Murdoch, who hated the movie.

As with *Kid A*, the reaction to *Fight Club* was divided along generational lines. Older viewers saw it as nihilistic and misogynist trash, while younger viewers saw the humor and connected with the film's extreme cynicism regarding the emptiness of consumer culture. While Radiohead would eventually align itself directly with the emerging anti-globalism movement, it's likely that many of the foot soldiers in that budding war were indoctrinated by listening to Tyler Durden preach the anti-corporate gospel in their friends' basements in the early '00s.

Let's say Thom Yorke had composed the score to *Fight Club*. Would that have changed how *Kid A* was received just one year later? Would music critics have teased out the thematic connections between the David Fincher movie and the Radiohead album? If so, would this have helped or hurt *Kid A*?

In time, *Fight Club* would be associated with extremist groups on both sides of the political divide, though far-right zealots like

Andrew Anglin, a notorious neo-Nazi provocateur and editor of white supremacist website *The Daily Stormer*, would be among the film's most notorious champions. The film's most lasting contribution to the lexicon is "snowflake," a putdown against sensitive liberals commonly used by the most odious dipshits on the Internet.

None of this is the fault of the people who made *Fight Club*. You can't blame the artists when the audience pulls a *Room 237* on your movie, and puts messages in there that you didn't intend. It's just that, sometimes, making an album is better.

You could, if so inclined, glean an actual ideology from *Fight Club* in a way you never could from *Kid A*. Pop music, unlike mainstream studio films, is the one major form of art in which the public is trained to *not* expect a linear storytelling structure. Songs are in fact usually worse when they spell out a clearly stated storyline. They can mean anything, everything, or nothing. It all depends on the listener. The meaning *has* to come from the audience.

If *Kid A* was merely evocative, *Fight Club* actually seemed prescriptive to some viewers. The quotable dialogue was a gospel, and the playful rebellions were a path forward. With *Kid A*, just figuring out what Thom Yorke was actually saying was usually enough.

When you're a person who thinks about music too much, you use it as a way to mark time. Even when the times that you're marking are far too somber and scary to be reduced to the terminology of rock music. Talking about world events in this way will inevitably make you sound shallow and even blinkered. And yet this is the vocabulary that some of us are stuck with.

Please know that I don't do this to downplay the significance of history. But I am deadly fucking serious when I say that the world never recovered from the era between *Kid A* and *Hail to the Thief.*

I guess we *think* we recovered. In the late 2010s, I read countless articles about how Donald Trump is the worst president in history, and represents the greatest threat to global democracy and freedom since, well, you-know-who from Germany. And I saw countless scandals perpetrated by this administration referred to as some kind of "-gate," a reference to the defining political scandal of the 1970s, Watergate.

But neither the present nor the distant past back in the twentieth century will ever be as traumatic to me as what occurred between the fall of 2000 and the late spring of 2003. In that time you have the 2000 US presidential election, September 11, and the wars in Afghanistan and Iraq. What links these four events is a breakdown in what might be described, simplistically but not inaccurately, as "a universally accepted version of the truth."

In the span of roughly thirty months, there was an election in which the man with fewer votes won because the Supreme Court had more justices aligned with his political party. Then there was the deadliest terrorist attack on American soil, which apparently had been foreseen by US intelligence officials but was never adequately addressed in advance. And *then* two wars were waged against countries we believed supported the organization responsible for that attack, though none of the attackers actually came from either of those countries. *All* of them were from the same different country, Saudi Arabia, which (of course) remained an American ally.

Oh, and there was that whole "this country has bombs that could kill all of us, so we must kill them" argument that proved to be a sham. Which means either the government actively lied to everybody in order to justify war, or the government was tricked into waging war under false pretenses. In either case, what was "real" was in fact *extremely fictional.*

That was just how it was in the early '00s. And you . . . accepted it.

How else do you process four world-changing events in such a small amount of time? Especially when, in the moment, your life doesn't seem to change all that much? You still get up, go to work, go home, get stoned, watch TV, and then drink too much at the same bar playing footage from Ground Zero on every screen. The madness is in the atmosphere. You breathe it in, and it's suddenly a part of you before you even realize it. You sucked on a lemon yesterday, but today it tastes merely like saliva.

Your way of life has been altered forever, but your *actual life* isn't over. And your brain won't let you dwell too much on what's been lost, because that will inevitably interfere with the process of staying alive. So, you adapt. The new normal becomes normal. You move on . . . even if you really don't, because *this is how things are now, and you can't escape it, only deny it.*

I didn't want to live in the present at that time. Nor did anybody else who I knew. After 9/11, you became addicted to watching the footage from Ground Zero all day and all night, just as you had once watched cable news all day and all night during the prolonged adjudication of the 2000 presidential election. But at some point you couldn't stand to take in so much of the new century. And the media, and VH1 specifically, understood this.

Near the end of 2002, the cable network debuted its *I Love the 80s* series. The show itself wasn't great—it was a junk-food compilation show in which semi-famous comedians and C-list actors reminisced about old stuff in a shallow "hey, remember this?" kind of way. Often, when looking back at an electro-pop oldie like the Human League's "Don't You Want Me," the panelists would simply just sing along with the song. That was about how deep *I Love the 80s* went. This wasn't criticism or analysis; it was basically a protoversion of Twitter, a scroll of familiar content that passed by at a steady clip with the purpose of perpetually micro-dosing your brain with feel-good, zero-substance stimuli.

For people of a certain generation—roughly anyone who was between the ages of eighteen and twenty-seven in the early '00s—getting high and watching *I Love the 80s* marathons on VH1 is a defining experience of those post-9/11, pre–social media years in the early '00s. Pure Soma for an overwhelmed mass consciousness. It not only took you out of the present, it also blocked out the future. All that was real was the never-ending patter about the pleasures of Atari, GoBots, *Webster,* and Rowdy Roddy Piper.

The Strokes' *Is This It* served a similar purpose. I wanted music that was directly connected to the rock 'n' roll I loved in the old century. You could play *Is This It* way too loud in the car at 3 A.M. when you were driving home from a place you shouldn't be driving from. Roll the windows down, stick out your left arm, feel the wind in your fingers, and imagine that you're Julian Casablancas whining about how your girlfriends don't understand, and your grandsons don't understand, and on top of this even *you* don't understand.

I can't hear the Strokes now without being instantly transported to that time when *nobody* understood what the hell was going on. Radiohead also takes me back, though I didn't play them all that much between 9/11 and the oncoming wars. Frankly, Radiohead was a little too much to take.

When you heard Radiohead, you were reminded that no matter how cool you looked in shades and a leather jacket, or how entertained you were by watching VH1 for five hours straight, it would not make the world any less frightening. The whole point of their records was that there were *no* answers, because the beasts at the door were vicious and defiantly post-logic. No rational argument or stirring protest song was going to quell them. They wanted your blood, and they were going to get it.

Radiohead ultimately made it impossible to buy into rock music as a viable means of salvation, which was not a truth I was willing to confront at that time.

When Radiohead's sixth album, *Hail to the Thief,* was released on June 9, 2003—three months after the US- and UK-led invasion of Iraq—the music press was eager to project a political agenda onto the album. The band seemed to invite this with an album title that (apparently) referenced the 2000 election, and a cover that stacked buzzwords upon buzzwords ("security," "aid," "oil") that anyone could recognize from the evening news. Yorke himself had also spoken out against the war, even as far back as the 9/11 concert. At an antiwar rally in England that preceded the album's release, he ripped the United States as a country "run by religious maniac bigots that stole the election."

And then there was the ferocious opening track, "2 + 2 = 5." After seeing the word "Orwellian" used to describe the past three albums, Radiohead finally caved and referenced *Nineteen Eighty-Four* directly. "It's the devil's way now," Yorke murmurs. "There's no way out." He then admonishes us four times that we have "not been payin' attention," a devastating act of CNN-shaming.

It was far more direct than anything on *Kid A* and *Amnesiac*, and nearly everyone who wrote about *Hail to the Thief* seized upon it immediately. In the context of the time, it seemed brave. Most of the songs that commented on 9/11 or the new wars were solidly pro-military and shamelessly jingoistic. This was typified by Toby Keith's "Courtesy of the Red, White, and Blue," in which the meathead country star promised to put a boot in the ass of Osama bin Laden for messin' with 'merica. In time, Neil Young would compose an entire antiwar record, *Living with War*, but in the immediate aftermath of the terrorist attacks even he put out a dunderheaded would-be anthem called "Let's Roll," a song about how "you've got to turn on evil" inspired by a man who attempted to stop the attackers on United Airlines Flight 93.

What wasn't noted as much about *Hail to the Thief* is that no other song on the album is as on-the-nose as "2 + 2 = 5." It reminds me of something Jeff Tweedy told me once about how the way albums are sequenced influences how they're written about. "The first songs on records always define that record," he said. For Wilco, if you put a mellow song first (like "Either Way" on *Sky Blue Sky*), it becomes the "mellow" album. If you put an experimental song first (like "Art of Almost" on *The Whole Love*), it becomes the "experimental" record.

For Radiohead, putting "2 + 2 = 5" first—a call made by Phil and Ed, who sequenced *Hail to the Thief*, not Thom—made it the political album. According to *Rolling Stone*, the album dove "headfirst into the dangers and challenges of living in a world run by cowboys, guns and money." For *New York* magazine, *Hail to the Thief* was great *in spite* of its politics, "which aren't so much leftist as deliberately murky."

Yorke himself subsequently seemed to come around to the latter point of view when he was interviewed about the album. "Having a son has made me very concerned about the future and about how things in the world are being steered, supposedly in my name," he told *Spin* when asked about the album's political leanings. "I wonder if our children will even have a future. But the trouble with your question—and we both know this—is that if I discuss the details of what I'm referring to in *Spin* magazine, I will get death threats. And I'm frankly not willing to get death threats, because I value my life and my family's safety. And that sort of sucks, I realize, but I know what is going on out there."

Besides, Yorke continued, *Hail to the Thief* was only *accidentally* political. "If the motivation for naming our album had been based solely on the U.S. election, I'd find that to be pretty shallow," he added in the *Spin* interview. "To me, it's about forces that aren't necessarily human, forces that are creating this climate of fear. While making this record, I became obsessed with how certain people are able to inflict incredible pain on others while believing they're doing the right thing. They're taking people's souls from them before they're even dead."

In another interview with the British edition of *GQ*, Yorke claimed that he wasn't "quite sure how we arrived at" the album title. "I don't think it's highly antagonistic, because out of this week's current context it sounds to me something from a fairytale," he added. "The political stuff is only there because of the lyrics, and the lyrics are only written that way because that's the way they came out."

Yorke described the album's gestation as coming out of a period in late 2001 when he was at home outside of Oxford after the tour for *Amnesiac*, with his girlfriend, Rachel, and their eight-month-old son, Noah. He would take two- or three-hour walks while listening to BBC News, gazing at the country scenery while also taking in press conferences from the Bush administration.

"Then I'd play this Penderecki tape in the car," he told the *Los Angeles Times*. "It makes *The Shining* soundtrack sound mild. An orchestra like a wall of amplifiers feeding back with this fragile cello in the middle. It fuses everything going on in your head, all that rattling debris."

What's clear when you read Yorke's own words at this time is that he didn't want to be Bono, a rock star/politician who has sit-downs with world leaders in order to hash out policies. Just talking about his political opinions in the context of promoting *Hail to the Thief* made him squirm.

The most uncomfortable interview conducted during this album cycle was with *Rolling Stone*'s David Fricke, who asked Yorke flat out, what do you think should have been done about Saddam Hussein? "In choosing to subvert the United Nations, to go around it, to treat it with complete contempt, we're entering a state of anarchy," he replied.

But what should the people in opposition do? Fricke wondered. "I don't have the answers," Yorke replied, with growing unease. "But the thing that keeps me awake at night is that my particular government is not answerable to the population."

Finally, Yorke threw up his hands. "When we were doing the record, I was trying hard not to get into any of this shit," he declared. "I don't want to be doing interviews about it. It's part of the absurdity, really, to even be answering questions, deconstructing the role of the U.N. Because shit, man, I don't want to know."

The most revealing part of the *Rolling Stone* interview—and
the key to understanding *Hail to the Thief*—came when Yorke
admitted that the album was in large part a reaction against the
Kid A period. On tour, they had turned those songs into loud
and proud *guitar-based* rock music. And they wanted that to carry
over to the album.

"When we talked about it, after the tour, we realized that we
didn't want to make any big creative leap or statement," he said.
"This is a good space we're in. We should carry on and enjoy it."

"2 + 2 = 5" is a crucial track on *Hail to the Thief*, but not as
an especially deep or forceful political statement. The first sound
you hear is Jonny Greenwood plugging in his guitar—if this were
any other band, it would have been mocked as a laughably obvious "back to basics" signifier. Because that's essentially how *Hail
to the Thief* was conceived. There were none of the constant deliberations of the *Kid A/Amnesiac* era. No Eno-esque experiments
to "disrupt" the band's normal way of working. They worked as a
live band again, and recorded quickly, like they did in the *Pablo
Honey* days.

"It's the way we work best," Yorke insisted to the *Los Angeles
Times*. "It was as if we'd been in hiding and now we've come out
in the open again. Direct music, quick, not thinking about it too
much, just letting things happen."

The writing and arranging process of *Hail to the Thief*, which
commenced in early 2002, was relatively relaxed. When the band
road-tested the material that summer on a short tour of Spain and
Portugal, Yorke was still trying out lyrics and tossing crumpled-up
rough drafts into the audience.

In September, Radiohead changed course again by decamp-
ing to Los Angeles, where much of the album was made. Sym-
bolically, this couldn't have been further removed from the

anti-stardom mantras of *Kid A* and *Amnesiac*. Radiohead had now inserted themselves directly into the belly of the beast. Though Yorke later explained to *Rolling Stone* that being so far from home kept everyone focused on the songs. "It was terrific, because we worked really hard. We did a track a day. It was sort of like holiday camp. We went to a couple of glamorous parties, which really helped. We don't have enough glamour in our lives. Too much news radio, not enough glamour."

All these years later, I haven't made up my mind about *Hail to the Thief*. Sometimes I think it's one of my least favorite Radiohead records; other times, I can't count a single track that I dislike. It was the hardest-rocking Radiohead album since *Pablo Honey*, and also the first Radiohead record since the debut that I liked immediately. The albums in between—*The Bends, OK Computer, Kid A*, and *Amnesiac*—all required some kind of warm-up period. But *Hail to the Thief* just seemed like an album that anybody who already liked Radiohead would *have* to like. It's a "greatest hits without the hits" album—an LP that most legacy acts get around to making eventually, in which you reiterate all of your previous incarnations in one place. R.E.M. did this brilliantly on *New Adventures in Hi-Fi*, David Bowie did it very well on *The Next Day*, and Talking Heads attempted it with mixed results on *Little Creatures*.

Hail to the Thief showed how quickly Radiohead had integrated the "radical" experiments on *Kid A* and *Amnesiac* into their core guitar-band aesthetic. "Where I End and You Begin" remade "The National Anthem," removed the horns, and turned it into a mesmerizing stoner-psych groove. "Myxomatosis," "Backdrifts," and "The Gloaming" similarly took the deconstructionist electronic excursions of the previous two albums and made them sound like relatively straightforward rock. Meanwhile, "Go to Sleep" reimagined "Karma Police" as grand, Zeppelin-esque folk rock with a hearty acoustic guitar lick that evoked "Over the Hills and Far Away."

The best song from *Hail to the Thief*, "There, There," derived from the *Kid A* period. Radiohead had debuted a rough early draft in a webcast from February of 2000. At that time, it was a muddy-sounding jam with an ominous vocal hook: "Just 'cause you feel it, doesn't mean it's there." A sentiment suited perfectly to the mood of *Kid A*, though by the time it was reworked for *Hail to the Thief* it evolved into one of the most thrilling guitar-based pieces in Radiohead's entire catalogue. I would even argue that the final two minutes and five seconds of "There, There"—the section that starts with "why so green and lonely?"—is *the* best piece of music this band has ever made. After trying to lay it down as a "live in the studio" track in L.A., Radiohead finally nailed it after returning to England and slowing down the menacing, Can-like groove in the front half, and building to the drama of the final section, which escalates to an overwhelming crescendo smashing through a wall of guitars.

Who could not be excited to hear Radiohead once again working in this mode? Even if it also seemed to repudiate the whole point of making *Kid A* in the first place?

On some level, *Hail to the Thief* felt reactionary. By then, it had become fashionable to "confess" that you hated Radiohead. Major media outlets like the *New York Post* ran stories about this phenomenon, as if choosing to dislike a popular and critically acclaimed rock band was a newsworthy form of cultural rebellion.

The gist of the anti-Radiohead takes was always the same—too artsy, too cerebral, too pretentious. Some of that had been in the air after the massive media response to *OK Computer*, but *Kid A* and then *Amnesiac* sealed the band's reputation as a kind of anti-visceral, elitist music that only smarty-pants dweebs cared about. As if on cue, Kid Rock confirmed this caricature in the video for his 2002 single "You Never Met a Motherfucker Quite Like Me," in which he reaches for a roll of toilet paper emblazoned with RADIOHEAD.

The irony could not have been lost on Radiohead—early in their career, they were dismissed as mindless grunge imitators, and now they were being called out for being emotionally distant wimps. *Hail to the Thief,* perhaps subliminally, felt like it was crafted as an antidote to that, a "we still know how to rock!" move that relegated the subversions of *Kid A* to a temporary tangent, rather than a bold path forward.

After *Hail to the Thief,* Radiohead didn't put out a new album for another four years, the longest gap between records at that time. Though four years or more would soon become standard for them. In the 2010s, they only put out two LPs, including their shortest and probably worst record, 2011's *The King of Limbs.*

From here on out, the members of Radiohead would drift a little from one another, focusing more and more on their own side projects, families, and personal lives. Though their bond remained intact, and eventually drew them back periodically to their familiar if fraught partnership, Radiohead would no longer be such a pivotal part of their lives. Nor would Radiohead be such a pivotal part of rock music, and nor would rock music be such a pivotal part of the culture.

With *Kid A,* Radiohead fought hard to find a place in the future. Now that the future had arrived, they would come to feel like a comforting remnant of a bygone time.

CHAPTER 8

BE YOURSELF ... BUT ON PURPOSE

In early 2019, I was fortunate to strike up an email correspondence with David Berman, the great songwriter and poet famous for fronting the indie-rock band Silver Jews.

At the time, Berman had not put out any new music in more than a decade. This diminished him in the larger music world, especially since his albums for many years weren't available on streaming services, which essentially rendered him invisible to 99 percent of music fans. But for the remaining 1 percent, Berman's untimely departure only heightened his mystique. He had retired his band, as he wrote in a note posted on the Silver Jews website, in protest over his father's long career as a lobbyist for corporations that sold guns, cigarettes, and other cultural destroyers. He pledged to do as much as he could to fix the damage his father had wrought, though it was unclear how not writing songs would play into that.

But that was then. Now Berman was preparing to return to public life. He had a new album, he explained in an introductory email, recorded under the name Purple Mountains. (He suspected that "Silver Jews" as a moniker wouldn't fly in more sensitive times.) While I had never met him, he felt compelled to reach out because he noticed that I had tweeted some nice things about Silver Jews in the past. Though, to be honest, I couldn't recall exactly what. Keep in mind: I have a bad habit of listening to songs that I love while I'm drinking, and then going on Twitter to share these fascinating developments. I'm sure I had been up one night a few years ago sipping whiskey and listening to *American Water*, and that's what brought David Berman to my email box.

If you know anything about Berman, you're also aware of how this story ends. In August of 2019, his body was found in a Brooklyn apartment. The self-titled Purple Mountains LP had come out just one month prior, to great critical acclaim. He was about to launch his first tour in many years. Instead, he hanged himself. He was fifty-two years old.

When someone dies, any encounter you had with that person instantly takes on great significance. You can't help but wonder if *this* conversation or *that* seemingly casual aside can explain why *it* happened. I won't do that with David Berman. However, there is one aspect of our encounters—which included a handful of emails and an intense ninety-minute phone interview—that has stuck with me. You could even say I'm "haunted" by it, though it's more curious than troubling.

It has to do with the question of when great artists start to suck.

Those are his words, not mine. Berman was obsessed with this question. He brought it up often in our emails, and it became one of the primary topics of our interview. "I guess when I was younger I always wondered, why do they always suck after thirty? After forty?" he said to me. "I don't know if I know the answer, but I know the solution."

For Berman, it had everything to do with time. When you're young, you have it to burn. And if you write and record songs for a living, you put almost all of that time into your art. If you have any talent at all, the benefit of putting so much time into one thing is that you produce the best work of your life. And you get a buzz from that creation that you can't get anyplace else.

But once you achieve greatness, what is the incentive to achieve it a second time? Or the tenth time? Or the forty-seventh time? At some point, the buzz just isn't there. If you manage to become successful, it's even harder to put so much of your time into that one thing.

As you get older, your perspective naturally changes. You still care about your art, but it's not the *only* thing you care about anymore. You might meet someone with whom you want to start a family. Now your partner and the children command most of your attention. These are new challenges in life, beyond the worlds of art you've already traversed and, in a sense, conquered.

To be great as a middle-aged artist, Berman concluded, "you have to put in a lot more time." Even if it comes at the expense of other parts of your life. Though for Berman, as he later explained to me, there were no other parts of his life. His marriage had recently ended, and he was living in a spare room at the offices of his record label, the Chicago-based indie Drag City. "I'm pretty solitary," he said.

I bring up this (tragic and depressing) anecdote because it helps to explain what happened to Radiohead in 2004.

That spring, the band embarked on the final leg of the *Hail to the Thief* tour, traveling from Japan to Australia to California, where they wrapped up the run at Coachella. While the tour doesn't look especially rigorous on paper, Thom Yorke later explained that these dates were brutal for the band.

"We flew the wrong way 'round the world," he told *Mojo*, "and ended up so jet-lagged, we never actually slept. Basically it was three or four weeks of constant sleep deprivation and illness. It was just shite. That tour was our last obligation and . . . it had stopped being fun."

After playing Coachella in May, Radiohead entered an unprecedented period of inactivity. No concerts to play, no album to make, no real reason to be a band. Their record deal with EMI had finally expired. They were now free agents without any obligations or deadlines. And, almost immediately, this newfound freedom started to erode Radiohead's very foundation.

For about nine months, Radiohead was dormant. The band members said later that they tended to their personal lives. By then, everyone was either married or entrenched in a long-term relationship. Each member of Radiohead also had at least two children. They now had the money and status to *not* tour or do any work at all. They could afford to put their time elsewhere.

Meanwhile Thom Yorke, who initially saw the lack of commitments as a blessing, was slowly being driven up a wall. He has been described by his partners in Radiohead as the band's most compulsively creative member, the one who is always scribbling down ideas and working through song ideas on his laptop. But now that his band had decided to unplug for an indefinite period, he found himself feeling incredibly depressed.

"I lost my confidence in all of it, I mean for about a year," he told the *New York Times*. "I used to bore my friends stupid in the pub."

Yorke had also battled depression in the aftermath of *OK Computer*, back when he was convinced that Radiohead had to dramatically remake itself into something utterly unlike Radiohead on their next album, *Kid A*. But this was different. In 1999, Radiohead almost broke up because they weren't sure if they had what it took to follow up the most significant album of their lives. But five years later, the fate of Radiohead again hung in the balance, because they were now the band that made *OK Computer* and *Kid A*. And, maybe, there was nothing else left to say. Perhaps it was now more important to focus more on life *outside* the band.

Of course, Radiohead did eventually reassemble, and they made one of their most beloved albums, 2007's *In Rainbows*. Though it proved to be a grind to create, taking more than two years. ("We'd all stopped to have kids. When we got back into the studio, it was just dead," Yorke told *Rolling Stone*.) In the process, they discovered there was still some unfinished business to address.

"I never felt we were one of the great bands, up there with The Smiths or R.E.M., you know," Ed O'Brien confessed to *Mojo* in 2008. "In my view, we've made three really great records, *The Bends*, *OK Computer* and *Kid A*. What we needed was another great record just to seal it."

Back in 2004, there was another crucial turning point for Radiohead that would extend beyond even *In Rainbows*. It was the beginning of projects outside of the band taking on greater significance, to the point of outnumbering Radiohead's rather meager output—just three studio albums in the latter half of the aughts and all of the '10s—during their "mid" period.

For Yorke, this meant finally getting to work on the debut solo LP that he had been contemplating since the *Kid A* era. The resulting album, *The Eraser*, would take the advancements of *Kid A* to their logical conclusion—instead of one of the world's greatest guitar bands twisting itself in knots in order to not sound like a guitar band, Yorke could literally dig out riffs and stray rhythm parts recorded by his bandmates and stored away on his laptop, and assemble them in any order he pleased, like a DJ rummaging through vinyl for the perfect sample.

In this way, *The Eraser* wasn't a true solo record at all, since Yorke often drew on instrumentals that had been performed by Radiohead. For the title track, he rearranged a series of piano chords played by Jonny Greenwood, and put them together into a new melody. The album's most Radiohead-like tune, "Black Swan"—which sounds like a close cousin of "I Might Be Wrong"—is built upon a groove performed by O'Brien and Phil Selway. Two other tracks, "And It Rained All Night" and "Harrowdown Hill," derived in some way from *Hail to the Thief*— the former was based on a highly discombobulated sample of "The Gloaming," the other was a demo that the band ultimately couldn't make work.

The album started as a diversion while Yorke waited to reconvene with Radiohead. Later, as he finished up *The Eraser* during breaks from the *In Rainbows* sessions, it was a way to feel productive as the band struggled to regain creative momentum after the prolonged break.

"There was a lot of me trying to pick myself up off the floor," he told the *New York Times*. "Because I really sort of dropped—what's the word? sunk—dropped down and went into this big lull and couldn't do anything."

Yorke subsequently explained that the title track was about the mass delusion that obscures the scariest existential threats in modern life, a callback to the recurring "this isn't happening" motifs of *Kid A*. There might have also been a sense for Yorke that his band was in danger of being erased, no matter the over-powering insistence of his creative impulses at the time. *The more you try to erase Thom, the more his ideas will appear on his own solo record.*

Yorke eventually enlisted Nigel Godrich to work as an editor and sounding board. It was Godrich who pushed Yorke to leave his voice relatively unadorned, a departure from the constant sonic fuckery that Yorke felt compelled to apply to his vocals after *OK Computer*. ("It annoys me how pretty my voice is," he griped to the *New York Times*.) Yorke originally hadn't planned on put-ting vocals on his new music at all, but he soon realized that his voice provided a through-line for the album that held the songs together.

"In the band he's always finding ways to bury himself," Godrich explained to the *Los Angeles Times*. "Being a big fan of his voice and his songs, I wanted to push that. It would have been sad if he'd just made an oblique record. But because it was predominantly electronic, I had a really good excuse to make his voice dry and loud."

For Yorke, *The Eraser* became a kinder, gentler *Kid A*, "some-thing really direct," as he told the *Los Angeles Times*, adding sardonically, "Someone might even understand it the first time around." While working with Radiohead in the studio had always been in some way torturous and time-consuming—which they tried to remedy by making *Hail to the Thief* so quickly, to their later chagrin—Yorke knocked out *The Eraser* in just seven weeks. He found that coming up with songs on his own was relatively easy—"so easy, you think it must be cheating," he said.

Upon its release in July of 2006, *The Eraser* naturally drew comparisons to *Kid A*. But as a piece of electronic music, it actually went much further than *Kid A* did, more closely resembling the Warp Records artists that enamored Yorke so much in 1998 and '99 than anything he worked up with the band.

As a metaphor for artistic reinvention, however, *The Eraser* was a far cry from *Kid A*. In the end, the significance of *Kid A* for Radiohead was the process they put themselves through in order to make it—they questioned everything, from their methods to their very reasons for being in a band at all. It was a self-inflicted trial by fire in which the relevance of Radiohead in the eyes of the members themselves was put on the line. The struggle was the point. Whereas with *The Eraser*, the chance to make music *without* the typical headaches of a Radiohead project was the draw.

No wonder it ultimately felt like cheating. When Yorke came out the other side, he found it was "suddenly easy to delineate how the band works as opposed to just me going off and doing my own thing," he said in an interview with *Mojo*. "Because it got to the point where I was sitting in a room across from Nigel and he'd be asking me, 'So how do we achieve this drum part you want?' And I frankly didn't have a clue."

Yorke spoke publicly on the inner workings of Radiohead during the press cycle for *The Eraser*, giving fans the clearest picture yet of his dynamic with Jonny Greenwood. To the *New York Times*, he admitted that he couldn't read or write music. "If someone lays the notes on a page in front of me, it's meaningless," he said. "Because to me you can't express the rhythms properly like that. It's a very ineffective way of doing it, so I've never really bothered picking it up." He also claimed that Jonny was "absolutely adamant that I should not learn to read music. He wants me to be the idiot savant."

Of course Greenwood had been dabbling in proper music notation since *The Bends*, when he wrote the string parts for "Fake Plastic Trees." Then, on *Kid A*, he worked with an orchestra for the first time. Several years after that, in 2003, he composed his first film score, for the documentary *Bodysong*. While not a proper solo album, *Bodysong* sounds very much like the ultimate sideman's record. The pieces don't really register as songs, but as evocative assemblages of incredible *sounds*—there's some heart-stopping classical music in the style of Krzysztof Penderecki, some *Bitches Brew* jazz, a bit of skronky guitar, and a whole lot of irregular electronic beats.

While *Bodysong* pre-dates *The Eraser* by three years, Greenwood was loath to describe it as a solo album. "I did music for a film but that's different to cobbling together 50 minutes of music with your name on it and expecting people to listen to it. That doesn't interest me at all," he told *Mojo*. Indeed, the music on *Bodysong*—as strange and wonderful as it is—is clearly intended to complement a primary voice. As he does with Yorke's songs, Greenwood works in the margins, adding myriad strange details and grace notes that keep listeners returning to what otherwise might be a conventional pop song.

While Yorke pushed himself toward even greater insularity on *The Eraser*, Greenwood eventually sought to enter a different kind of collaboration. In writer-director Paul Thomas Anderson, he found his surrogate, cinematic Thom Yorke. "I knew there were arrangements that he had done within those Radiohead songs that obviously said he could do more than just play guitar in a band," Anderson later told the *New York Times*. "And I thought, If the opportunity arises, I bet he could do something interesting on a film score. I was just sort of waiting for the opportunity."

The first score that Greenwood wrote for Anderson, for 2007's *There Will Be Blood*, is—along with *The Eraser*—the greatest music that any member of Radiohead has made outside of the group. Greenwood, who went on to score PTA's next three films, likened their partnership to a band, perhaps because that's all he had ever known going back to his teen years in On a Friday. He was comfortable with his role as a fixer who helps bring to life the musings of a genius misanthrope obsessed with how capitalism and technology are ruining the environment and the greater human spirit. Jonny had done it with Thom on *Kid A*, and now he was making *There Will Be Blood*, a turn-of-the-century morality tale that begins in 1898—one hundred years before the end of the *OK Computer* tour—with Kid PTA.

As a composer, Greenwood naturally loved how loud Anderson lets the music play in his films, sometimes even allowing the score to drown out his own dialogue. In *There Will Be Blood*, Anderson gives Greenwood a grand entrance at the start of the movie, an opening on an ominous mountain—add snow, and it would directly evoke the cover of *Kid A*—set to the Penderecki-like squalls of the score. Soon, we'll see Daniel Plainview digging his well and making his fortune. This is a man already driven mad by his own greed—when he breaks his legs after falling down the well, he drags himself on his back over that very mountain in order to have his fortune affirmed.

A century later, the world that men like Daniel Plainview created will seem so perverse and gross and frankly terrifying to an

English rock band that they will be driven to make cut-and-paste protest songs inspired by the slow suffocation of global commerce.

When I watch *There Will Be Blood* and hear Greenwood's music, I imagine I'm hearing part of a Radiohead album, just as I do whenever I put on *The Eraser*. Sometimes I imagine putting them *together*, the laptop record of chopped-and-reconfigured Radiohead riffs with the Penderecki homages creeping in from the fringes. The great, lost Radiohead album.

The LP that Radiohead eventually put out, *In Rainbows*, doesn't really sound like that, of course. It is instead the most melodic, effervescent, and lived-in music they've ever made. As natural as breathing in and out, it flows out of the speakers like rays of light. It is, in many ways, the yang to *Kid A*'s yin, as warm and welcoming as its predecessor is cold and foreboding. In time, *In Rainbows* would come to overshadow *Kid A* for many Radiohead fans.

This is based purely on anecdotal evidence, but it has been so overwhelmingly true in my experience that I'm inclined to take it as broadly true: *In Rainbows* is the consensus choice for "best" Radiohead album. This is especially true for Millennials and Generation Z, who no doubt flock to *In Rainbows* because it was the first Radiohead album that was "theirs." They were too young to scour the Internet for illegal downloads of *Kid A* back in 2000, and *The Bends* and *OK Computer* already sounded "too '90s" by the mid-aughts. But *In Rainbows*, as music and a *moment*, hit that generation just right.

If *Kid A* rescued Radiohead from being known strictly as a '90s band, *In Rainbows* ensured that they would belong to multiple generations. The uniqueness of this achievement can't be overstated. Virtually no other band from Radiohead's peer group was able to pull it off. While there are fans of Pearl Jam, Sonic Youth, and R.E.M. from younger generations, it's generally understood that those are Gen-X bands. Their classic work was released during a relatively concentrated period of time, usually over the course of a decade. For Radiohead, there's a similar span of time between *OK Computer* and *In Rainbows*. And yet that decade, which straddles two centuries, also represents a very long bridge between two completely different eras. There was no guarantee that a twenty-one-year-old in 2007 was going to care about *OK Computer* and *Kid A*. But *In Rainbows* connected that person to those records.

The age of this hypothetical music fan is important. For a band to matter to a particular generation, they have to put out a culturally significant record when those people are between the ages of eighteen and twenty-two. *OK Computer* will probably always be my favorite Radiohead record, because it dropped when I was about to turn twenty. The micro-generation of music fans slightly younger than me, which includes the first group of kids for whom it was common to have email addresses and access to Napster in high school, had *Kid A*. And the kids who came of age during the last great indie-rock boom had *In Rainbows*. None of their contemporaries could pull that off for Millennials. But Radiohead somehow made it across that twentieth-/twenty-first-century, Gen-X/Millennial divide. Which is why, a full decade after *In Rainbows*, Radiohead remained one of the only rock bands on Earth that could credibly headline an otherwise rock-averse festival like Coachella. What other band still seems like they belong to everybody?

The wonder of *In Rainbows* is that it proved to be as difficult to make as any Radiohead album. The record's sweet lightness belied the torturous two-years-plus ordeal required to finish it. Ultimately, *In Rainbows* took about as long to complete as *Kid A* and *Amnesiac*. Though, unlike those records, the struggle over *In Rainbows* played out in public, via the band's own *Dead Air Space* blog and interviews that Yorke conducted while promoting *The Eraser*. Yorke's first solo record was itself a kind of subtweet about how difficult it was to get anything done in Radiohead.

"We lost all momentum and it's very, very difficult to get momentum back," Yorke complained to the *New York Times* in 2006. "When I say momentum, I don't just mean the physically working every day, I mean just hanging out and playing each other music and swapping ideas and stuff. It's something that you take for granted until it's gone. And then you're like: 'What's wrong? There's something wrong here.'"

Whereas British music magazines were forced to dispatch reporters to Oxford to literally knock on doors in order to collect any stray scrap of information about *Kid A* and *Amnesiac*, Radiohead fans had a clear picture of just how much trouble Radiohead was having in the studio with *In Rainbows* long before they heard the record. The accounts from various press reports proved to be more or less consistent: They started work in mid-February of 2005, after taking the back half of 2004 off. The songs that Yorke brought in excited the band. Ed especially felt moved by the new material, which was uniquely romantic, even sexy. (Yorke would later describe them as his "seduction songs.") "It was the first time in a long while that I felt really engaged with the lyrics," O'Brien told *Mojo* in 2008.

The idea right away was to make a lean record with ten or eleven songs, a reaction to the overstuffed *Hail to the Thief*. The tunes were simple and heartfelt, lending themselves to straightforward interpretations. There would seemingly be no need for the endless deliberations and mind games of 1999 and 2000 . . . except Radiohead found themselves slipping back into their old habits.

The initial excitement that the band felt in February soon faded as they rehearsed endlessly over the next several months. In time, their fragile sense of self-confidence as a band was shattered. The old demon from the *Kid A* era eventually returned— they could sense that they worked best when they simply plugged in and worked through the songs live, and yet when they played back the songs they recorded that way, it sounded basic and obvious, even dull.

And then there was the momentum issue. They didn't *need* to make an album, or do anything else as a band, at this point. With *Kid A*, Radiohead found that having an open-ended deadline and considerable resources to make whatever album they wanted—which, given that memories of the rushed sessions for *Pablo Honey* and *The Bends* were still fresh, was a genuine luxury—eventually worked against them. But at least they had the motivation of youth and the drive to prove all of the people who thought they could never top *OK Computer* wrong. With *In Rainbows*, the only motivation was whether they really wanted to do it *again*. And maintaining a legacy will never be as compelling as building one.

They didn't even know what to actually *do* with this music, assuming they could ever get their act together and finish it off. They still didn't have a record deal, and while they weren't sure they even wanted one, they also didn't know what to do as an alternative. "We were having endless debates, spending entire afternoons talking about, 'Well, if we do something, how do we put it out?'" Yorke said later. "It just became this endless and pointless discussion. Because in our dreams, it would be really nice to just let off this enormous stink bomb in the industry."

By October, Yorke was moved—as he often was during this period—to rant melodramatically on the *Dead Air Space* blog. "We're splitting up," he wrote. "It's all shit. We're washed up, finished."

Of course, Radiohead wasn't finished, nor was *In Rainbows* done with being a frustrating slog. Rather than use Nigel Godrich, who was busy helping Yorke with *The Eraser* along with working with Beck on *The Information*—an album that I, along with most people, have played exactly once—they had asked Mark "Spike" Stent in December '05 to listen to what they had been working on. And Stent, whose résumé included records by U2, Björk, and Massive Attack, confirmed their worst fears, according to O'Brien, who recalled him flatly declaring, "The sounds aren't good enough."

So now Spike Stent was on board as a producer as Radiohead entered early 2006, a full year after they started working on their seventh album. With Stent, they laid down early versions of future *In Rainbows* tracks like "Bodysnatchers," "Nude," and "Weird Fishes/Arpeggi." But still, they were dissatisfied. "I've been fucking tearing my hair out," Yorke fumed on the blog that March. Eventually, Stent would exit the project.

Radiohead was in serious trouble.

From the outside, little about the making of *In Rainbows* makes sense. Why was this, of all Radiohead albums, arguably the hardest for them to make? It wasn't some radical sonic reinvention for the band. The songs themselves appear to have been in place well before they were officially laid down. It seems like Radiohead had a great record in their grasp for months, even years before *In Rainbows* was finally released. And yet . . . they couldn't figure it out.

For the longest time I couldn't fathom any of it. And then I remembered one of the core foundations of my personal philosophy on life, the 1986 Martin Scorsese film *The Color of Money*.

I would never call *The Color of Money* the best Scorsese movie. It's not even the fifth best. Nor is it the best movie in which Paul Newman plays the hard-luck, streetwise pool player "Fast" Eddie Felson. (That would be 1961's *The Hustler.*) But it is a movie I think about a lot, because Newman spouts so many quotable lines that I've come to take as valuable life advice. For instance, when Fast Eddie is teaching his headstrong young protégé Vincent Lauria (Tom Cruise) about how to take a dive in a game in order to win more money in the long run, he says, "Sometimes when you lose, you win."

Sometimes when you lose, you win. That's about as close as you can get to summing up the meaning of life while also talking about how to scam suckers at billiards.

The *Color of Money* quote that pertains to Radiohead's predicament at the time of *In Rainbows* occurs when Newman is trying to explain that Vincent has to be self-aware about his weaknesses and eccentricities, so that he can use them to his advantage when he's hustling people. "He's got to learn how to be himself," Eddie says, "but on purpose."

That had been Radiohead's problem since the *Kid A* era. They didn't know how to be themselves, but on purpose. On *Kid A*, they were deliberately trying to *not* be themselves. They changed how they worked, and they subtracted the elements of their music that were most recognizable and subsequently co-opted by a legion of copycats. Though when they got on the road they found the songs opened up in new and surprising ways when they played them like the same old Radiohead.

On *Hail to the Thief*, they overcorrected, working swiftly as a live unit without stopping to consider whether they really needed to put "The Gloaming" *and* "We Suck Young Blood" on the same record, or *any* record. For *In Rainbows*, they finally had to finish the process of self-discovery that began several years earlier with *Kid A*. "I suppose we were paying the price for not taking the pain on *Hail to the Thief*," a reflective Colin Greenwood told *Mojo* in 2008. "As this project progressed, we realized there are no short cuts to the process being exciting for us."

As is usually the case with Radiohead, the path toward a solution started by going back on the road in the summer of 2006, including a headlining appearance at Bonnaroo that would be remembered by fans and the band members themselves as an all-time gig. Six songs that ended up on *In Rainbows* were played that night: "15 Step," "Weird Fishes/Arpeggi," "Videotape," "Nude," "Bodysnatchers," and "House of Cards," with the latter two numbers showing up in each of the two encores. That's basically the meat of the record, performed pretty much exactly as they would appear on *In Rainbows*. (I actually prefer the ominous live version of "Videotape" from Bonnaroo to the take on the album.)

The audience's response to the new material is audibly enthusiastic; fans in many cases already knew the songs from other concerts bootlegged online, as they had during the early *Kid A* shows. Radiohead should have gone home from these shows feeling like they were ready to lay down a classic. But they were instead driven to tinker even more.

"To be brutally honest," O'Brien later admitted, "the problem about playing these songs live is that we were bored with them. We played them 80 times live or so, and we'd rehearsed them to death. It just didn't happen when we got back into the studio initially."

This time, at least, they had Godrich back in the fold. Yorke had been lobbying to bring him back via his press interviews for *The Eraser*, while also hinting that his close relationship with Godrich—along with the suspicion that using him again was the "safe" choice—was a problem for the rest of the band. But by the fall of 2006, it was clear that Radiohead needed help from their old collaborator, who in turn suggested that they ship off to a condemned, possibly haunted mansion in the English countryside—"literally an old country pile," as O'Brien put it—a gambit that had previously worked for the band on *OK Computer* and *Kid A*.

This practice of stealing away to some house outside of the hustle and bustle of civilization to create your masterpiece evokes the old myths about Bob Dylan and the Band knocking out *The Basement Tapes* at Big Pink in upstate New York. There's also an element of the *Rocky* movies, in which the beleaguered champ goes into the mountains to haul boulders through the snow in order to get back into fighting shape.

For Radiohead, the fight to get out of one's head remains the most enduring problem of their creative lives. And anything they could do to put themselves out of the mode of perpetual analyzation, and just *be*, was worth pursuing. For Yorke, in particular, this would prove key for *In Rainbows*. "The more you absorb yourself in the present tense, the more likely that what you write will be good," he insisted upon the album's release.

The pivotal track in that regard proved to be "Reckoner," a snaky, rattling track with a ghostly, John Frusciante–inspired guitar lick and a gorgeous, soaring vocal by Yorke. The song was first performed live during the *Amnesiac* tour, at a concert in George, Washington, that subsequently became a popular bootleg among fans. Though this version of "Reckoner"—a violent, snarling rocker far heavier than anything on *Kid A* or *Amnesiac*—wound up being an entirely different song from the "Reckoner" that appeared on *In Rainbows*. (Yorke later released it as a solo single called "Feeling Pulled Apart by Horses," which is also an apt description of what it sounds like.)

After the 2006 tour, Radiohead decided to revive "Reckoner," adding a new coda, and then another part. Finally, they discarded the original song altogether. For Yorke, this stood out as the band learning how to live in the moment. "It's what sticks that I'm after and that happened a few times while making this," Yorke said. "I try and do that thing where it's sort of automatic, that whatever comes out comes out and try not to censor it too much."

"Reckoner" is indicative of the overall shift that Radiohead's music took with *In Rainbows*. Unlike the classic songs from the '90s, or the attempts at reviving that sound on *Hail to the Thief*— "we were trying to do what people said we were good at," Yorke later admitted to *Mojo*—the songs on *In Rainbows* rarely build to some dramatic climax. There are no crescendos in "Reckoner," "House of Cards," "Weird Fishes," or "All I Need." They appear, they move throughout the world, and then they fade out. They live out the same arc that human beings do, which is why they feel and sound so natural and organic. They aren't telegraphing the moments where you're supposed to feel a surge of adrenaline or an unstoppable compulsion to weep. There is enough space and air in this music to put whatever you want into it. While *In Rainbows* isn't ambient music, it does have a similar atmospheric sensation, creating a sonic world that doesn't intrude on that of the listener, but rather complements it, like a warm blanket or a bottle of red wine.

This wasn't the Radiohead of *Kid A*, fighting with itself for months upon months in order to become something new and revolutionary. This was Radiohead being themselves, but on purpose.

CHAPTER 9

EVERYBODY WANTS
TO BE A FRIEND

They sounded like Joy Division, kind of.

More accurately, they were like the Cure if Robert Smith had affected a half-decent Ian Curtis impersonation. A description that could apply to at least 12,000 post-punk bands from the UK that have formed in the past forty years. But for Aerial FX, their sonic CV was especially problematic.

In 1980 Joy Division was freshly defunct, a busted band in the wake of Curtis's suicide on the eve of their first American tour. Right when Joy Division met its tragic end, Aerial FX was freshly born, though the outside world was mostly indifferent to the latter development. In Oxford, however, they were definitely the new synth-rock/sad-guy/spooky-vibes band to watch.

Between 1980 and '82, they put out three 7-inches with names like *So Hard* and *Take It from Here* and *Instant Feelings*. The generic titles properly conveyed the contents, though Aerial FX did manage to land a record deal with EMI. Their first full-length, 1982's *Watching the Dance*, isn't bad. The first and best track, "Out of the Window," has a pretty good bass line, drums that sound like trash cans falling down a reverb-coated staircase, and sparkly guitars that glower like forlorn thunderstorms. A clever record-label executive would have tried to market them as the latest world-conquering New Romantics band. But Aerial FX didn't have the flash, glamour, or hooks for that designation. So *Watching the Dance* came and went like pretty much every other OK UK post-punk band. Ultimately, Aerial FX did not wind up on a party yacht with Simon Le Bon. Instead, the debut LP bombed and they broke up soon after.

The band's two principals, Chris Hufford and Bryce Edge, drifted back to the real world. In 1987, they invested in an Oxford-area real estate development called Georgetown. A complex that included residential homes and business spaces, Georgetown piqued the interest of Hufford and Edge, in part, because it also included a 24-track recording studio, which they would later dub Courtyard Studios. Maybe they could keep on making music while making ends meet with the business. The studio was a significant improvement over the 8-track setup that Hufford had installed in a rented barn that regularly drew noise complaints from the neighbors. Maybe the dreams of Aerial FX didn't have to be over after all.

Only, Georgetown proved to be a money pit for Hufford and Edge. Soon, they were forced to sell off their land. By 1990, all that was left was their recording studio. Since their music careers were no more successful than their real estate business, the partners were persuaded to invite local groups to record there. Edge handled the business, and Hufford functioned as an in-house producer. Most of these groups have since been lost to time, though the duo did manage to work with a promising dream pop act, Slowdive, whose 1991 debut *Just for a Day* was produced by Hufford.

But fate had bigger things in store for the leftover remnants of Aerial FX. On August 8, 1991, Hufford somehow made his way to Jericho Tavern to catch a show by On a Friday. It's not completely certain why he was there—it's been said that he heard the band's demo, or that he simply happened to be there by chance while showing the members of Slowdive around town. What's important is that Hufford had one of those Jon Landau–esque "I've seen rock's future and it's Radiohead" moments. More than anything, he was knocked out by Yorke's voice. This was not another Ian Curtis wannabe. This guy was *it*.

Initially, Hufford was simply interested in hustling On a Friday into his studio. In October, they recorded at Courtyard what became known as the "Manic Hedgehog" tape, which included rough versions of three future *Pablo Honey* tracks: "You," a rocked-up "Thinking About You," and my precious "I Can't." But after Hufford and Edge also helped On a Friday to distribute the tape, they started to seem like potential managers. Fortuitously, a record label was already interested in On a Friday: Colin Greenwood that summer had passed along an old demo tape to EMI's Keith Wozencroft, a sales representative who fell under the spell of the song "Stop Whispering" and raved about it to the label's A&R department. From there, Hufford and Edge called on their old contacts from the Aerial FX days to move On a Friday up the flagpole.

And the rest, as we've already recounted, is history.

Hufford and Edge haven't been as publicly associated with Radiohead as other manager-band combinations, like Paul McGuinness with U2 or Jefferson Holt and Bertis Downs with R.E.M. But they've been part of the team since the beginning of the band's rise, providing the kind of stability that long-running rock bands require in order to go the distance.

They also came up with one of the most famous ideas associated with Radiohead—"pay what you want."

It occurred during the tediously slow gestation of *In Rainbows*, when the band's managers had little to do but get high and hatch harebrained, semi-socialist business schemes. One day they were stoned and ruminating over the fact that every Radiohead album since *Kid A* had leaked. What if they posted the next Radiohead LP—assuming the band eventually finished the damn thing— themselves as a download? After all, they were technically free agents now, so they certainly *could* do whatever they wanted. Why not this?

Eventually, Radiohead would put out *In Rainbows* in an unprecedented fashion—at least for a band as rich and famous as they were—making it available for whatever fans were willing to pay. Gone, it seemed, was all of the usual machinery that accompanied the release of a big-time rock record. There was no extensive pre-release promotional campaign, no marketing tie-ins with big-box retailers, or anything else that was traditionally implemented to turn out rock-'n'-roll hype.

A generation earlier, in the same summer of 1991 that Chris Hufford was first blown away by Thom Yorke, Guns N' Roses had teased their outrageously bloated pair of double albums, *Use Your Illusion I* and *II*, with a video for the song "You Could Be Mine" that was also featured in the year's most outrageously bloated summer blockbuster, *Terminator 2: Judgment Day*. That was how popular rock bands used to do things. But with *In Rainbows*, Radiohead sought to realize the digital utopianism that had characterized the release of *Kid A*.

In 2000, much of Radiohead's audience was conditioned to view the Internet as the primary avenue for accessing music, along with news and conversation with fellow fans. While many of us were already online in order to steal music, Radiohead was among the first bands to legitimize the web as the place where you now lived as a music fan.

As the aughts unfolded, the music industry came to treat selling music online first as a novelty, and then as a potential salvation as brick-and-mortar stores rapidly disappeared. But for Radiohead and their community of fans, the Internet still seemed like a space that could potentially exist *beyond* capitalism, a "no logos" DMZ in which the musicians and the audience could communicate without a corporate intermediary. It was just you and Radiohead, sharing this music. *In Rainbows* felt like the culmination of this *Kid A*–era idealism.

About two out of five people who downloaded the album during the first month paid for it. That's not counting the millions of people who just downloaded it illegally elsewhere. But the people who did pay contributed an average of $6 per album—factoring in the freeloaders, that was still $2.26 per record, which was more than Radiohead would have likely made had they stayed with their record label, EMI.

The world learned about the release strategy for *In Rainbows* just ten days before it appeared online, via a nonchalant blog post written by Jonny. But Hufford and Edge had been strategizing for months, while also negotiating a possible reup deal with EMI.

(One of the label contacts regularly in touch with Radiohead's management at the time was Wozencroft, who no doubt viewed his discovery of Radiohead on EMI's behalf as a feather in his cap.)

This behind-the-scenes wheeling and dealing wasn't reported until years later, long after the mythology of *In Rainbows* and "pay what you want" had become the latest foundational text in the church of Radiohead. In retrospect, the band's motivations for essentially giving away *In Rainbows* might not have been quite as pure as they originally seemed.

For starters, Radiohead was pissed that EMI and Terra Firma, the private-equity group that acquired the label in 2007 for $4.7 billion, wouldn't give them back their own catalogue. Subsequent press reports painted Radiohead's *In Rainbows* gambit as a fuck-you move. This, in turn, prompted a fuck-you move from EMI's new chairman, Guy Hands. (Guy Hands, surprisingly, is not a fictional name for an entertainment-industry executive.) After Radiohead departed EMI and put out *In Rainbows* online, EMI countered by releasing a box set of the band's albums in time for the Christmas season. The following year, they put out a two-disc greatest-hits album, a low blow to a band that prided itself on staying relevant and compilation-averse.

"They publicly go out and humiliate us. My view was, 'Fine!'" Hands later reasoned. "I said, 'We have a bank that is staring us down and now they have basically told us to eff off, I don't think we have a huge amount of reasons to be nice to them."

As for Yorke, the archival box set—which Radiohead did not have any input on—"fucking ruined my Christmas," he complained.

If Radiohead had truly set out to make a grand statement about how the old, corrupt, twentieth-century-berthed record industry had overstayed its welcome and finally had to be ushered out, they certainly had the proper origin story for it. But as always with this band, there was discomfort with making too-direct, on-the-nose proclamations about the romanticism of *In Rainbows* in terms of the larger music industry.

"If I die tomorrow, I'll be happy that we didn't carry on working within this huge industry that I don't feel any connection with," Yorke told *Rolling Stone*. "But the idea wasn't to make a big, significant statement. I mean, we knew it would be messing with things a little bit. But we just wanted to get the album to people who'd been waiting patiently for four years. I really thought it would be a splash in a little pond, and I was surprised at how much the media picked up on it."

Jonny Greenwood echoed Yorke's noncommittal "splash in a little pond" characterization, claiming that the "idea really was boredom-driven. Just about avoiding the old."

But even if Radiohead chose to downplay what it had done with *In Rainbows*, there was a brief moment when it seemed like things might be different now. As skeptics were quick to point out, selling an album directly to fans without the benefit of a record label to promote and distribute the music was a luxury only a band with a decade and a half of major corporate-label support like Radiohead could manage. But while that was true, the Internet was also still young enough that the *idea* that other major acts could follow Radiohead's example didn't seem beyond the realm of possibility. These were, after all, the days when the eventual destruction of the record industry was almost a foregone conclusion. Why wouldn't bands of Radiohead's stature now exist as independent nation-states in the rock world, performing on an arena-band scale while operating essentially as a mom-and-pop business?

It didn't work out that way, of course. The same month *In Rainbows* came out, in October 2007, a new company launched in Sweden: Spotify. With *Kid A*, it was unclear for a while whether Radiohead had made the first album of the twenty-first century or the last album of the twentieth. But the advent of Spotify made it abundantly obvious that *In Rainbows* was not the beginning of a new dawn for how rock bands and audiences would interact, but rather the end of the era in which a single rock album could act as a focal point for the online world.

Radiohead's solution to piracy was to put out *In Rainbows* as a surprise release, so that it wouldn't leak. This worked for approximately a minute or two after the album came out, at which point it was swiftly pirated anyway. There was also the idea that allowing listeners to pay what they want would implant a philosophical debate into their minds. Now they would have to decide how much compensating the creators of the music that they love was worth to them.

The *In Rainbows* release strategy was, clearly, the sort of fix that only artists would come up with. Spotify meanwhile was a mechanical shark created by technicians and businesspeople that operated solely on the logic of supply and demand. What the company was banking on was that piracy had become too much work for the average listener—the time spent hunting down legitimate download links that wouldn't crash your computer, plus the hassle of storing all of those files, had become an inconvenience. What if instead you could pay a nominal fee—or choose to just sit through advertising—to hear pretty much *anything* you could want?

Spotify wasn't about *one* album, but *all* albums. Set aside the fact that nobody wants to hear *all* albums—the *idea* of all-points access is as irresistible as an all-you-can-eat buffet. Spotify made piracy obsolete because it understood that listeners were not going to respond to appeals to their morality, like Radiohead tried with *In Rainbows*. But they would care instinctively about preserving their time and money.

The problem for Radiohead was that a moral philosophy really did matter as a core component of their music—that was certainly true for *In Rainbows*, and also for *Kid A*. The idea all along was to have a one-to-one relationship with the audience, to create a sphere in which everyone was fully human and accounted for. But Spotify reduced all music to bits of data that may or may not be discovered with the help of a computerized algorithm. This wasn't a safe space for Radiohead or any other band to commune with its people. Spotify was defiantly, and conveniently, *anti-human*. There were no people here, just avatars and mechanized playlists.

At the time of *Kid A*, Radiohead had been ahead of the curve on the Internet, embracing the possibilities and implicitly shaming the anti-web alarmists in the music industry. But in the age of Spotify, they suddenly become the holdouts. For years, you couldn't stream Radiohead's music anywhere. At issue was the inadequate compensation that streaming services paid out to artists. But there was also, it seemed, a palpable, lingering bitterness over what had been squandered over the course of the aughts, from *Kid A* to *In Rainbows*.

"When we did the *In Rainbows* thing what was most exciting was the idea you could have a direct connection between you as a musician and your audience. You cut all of it out, it's just that and that. And then all these fuckers get in the way, like Spotify suddenly trying to become the gatekeepers to the whole process," Yorke said in 2013. "It's like this mind trick going on, people are like 'with technology, it's all going to become one in the cloud and all creativity is going to become one thing and no one is going to get paid and it's this big super intelligent thing.' Bullshit."

Eventually, Radiohead gave in, and allowed its albums to be played on Spotify and elsewhere. The fuckers had gotten in the way and they weren't going to move.

But old dreams die hard. Yes, there was the issue of artists being paid. But for those of us in the audience, a certain spirit had also shifted. In 2000, you went on the Internet to learn about *Kid A*. It's where you heard the album stream, downloaded the concert bootlegs, and read the album reviews. It was a tool that you used to make your life better.

But by the end of the aughts, it seemed like the opposite had been true all along: *Kid A* had really just been a way to get you on the Internet. *The tool was now using you.* You didn't live there. You were stuck there. And there was no place else left to go.

Radiohead did not put out any new music in 2010, the year of *Kid A*'s tenth anniversary. Outside of a one-off show performed in January in Los Angeles, a fundraiser for victims of the Haiti earthquake, they did not tour either. But they were involved in one genuinely great musical moment that felt like a sequel to *Kid A*, even as it revived and reimagined the track that functions as the antithesis of *Kid A* in Radiohead's discography.

It occurred in the trailer for *The Social Network*, David Fincher's film about the early days of Facebook and the moral compromises of its founder, Mark Zuckerberg, that premiered theatrically in the United States almost exactly ten years to the day after the release of *Kid A*, on October 1, 2010. While the movie is fantastic and probably my favorite film of the 2010s, I'm not sure if it ever topped that trailer. Or, to be more exact, the first fifty-two seconds of the trailer.

When the song starts it sounds familiar but not overly so. You know you should be able to place it but you can't . . . quite do it. A classical piano has been put in the place of gently ringing guitars. A choir has replaced the solitary singer who does not belong here. But the music is still beautiful and unmistakably foreboding. On the screen, we see images that appear to have been taken from Facebook. A baby's feet. A wedding photo. A group of friends dancing at a party. A woman silhouetted against a sunset. Eventually, you notice that the choir of female voices on the soundtrack are singing some instantly familiar lines: *I don't care if it hurts / I wanna have control* . . .

Even after Radiohead got their full due, a decade after the fact, for the genius of *Kid A*, they still couldn't totally escape the reach of "Creep." This version was recorded by Scala & Kolacny Brothers, a Belgian women's choir under the direction of conductor Stijn Kolacny and pianist Steven Kolacny, and originally released in 2006 on the album *On the Rocks,* which also included covers of songs by Nirvana, Kylie Minogue, and Muse. I understand that this might seem corny on paper. The Somber, Unconventional Cover of a Rock Classic is now a tired staple of movie trailers. It's pretty much required now that if you have a thriller or a horror movie to sell, you have to score the teaser with a cover of Modern English's "I Melt with You" or Tears For Fears' "Everybody Wants to Rule the World" that's been made to sound like an Evanescence power ballad from 2002.

And then there's the matter of using *Radiohead* covers in films and TV shows in order to denote a chilling warning about technology and the terrifying effects it will have on the future. In the

2010s, there was a mini-trend of using "Exit Music (For a Film)" as a powerful emotional payoff for dystopian TV shows like *Black Mirror* and *Westworld*, which also utilized unusual reinventions of other Radiohead tracks, like "Fake Plastic Trees," "Motion Picture Soundtrack," and "No Surprises."

I acknowledge all of this in order to reiterate that in 2010, in the trailer for *The Social Network*, the choral version of "Creep" *nevertheless* works beautifully. Watching it now, you can link the solipsism of the lyric to something larger about how social media has enabled "I wish I was special"–style self-absorption and projected it throughout the entire world, in all facets of public life, from your phone to the White House. If you *want* something to be true, you can *imagineer* it, to use one of the more odious examples of corporate-speak.

The film pulls a similar trick, connecting the feelings of loneliness and alienation felt by Zuckerberg (Jesse Eisenberg) to his ambitions for a site in which relationships were digitized, commodified, and, ultimately, weaponized. Of course, Eisenberg is a lot more charming than the real Zuckerberg, a frightfully robotic and cold-blooded man who at times resembles the crash-test dummy on the cover of *The Bends*. And *The Social Network* came out six years too early to address the most destructive part of Facebook's legacy, the Russian interference that undermined the 2016 US presidential election.

When *Kid A* was released in 2000, and the world proceeded to change so dramatically in the next several years, the assumption was that dystopia would be imposed on us from outside forces. The enemies were George W. Bush and Fox News and Halliburton and the untold millions of people *out there* who supported these ghouls. You didn't know them personally but you were convinced they had it in for you and anyone else who questioned their authority. But in the 2010s, we learned that these evils were not actually *imposed* at all. We all signed up for them of our own volition. On Facebook, *we* want to have control. Because *we* want others to notice when we aren't around. We *want to be special. So fucking special.*

So we have willingly participated in a platform that has turned information—once the lifeblood of the Internet—into misinformation, a devastating cudgel used to destroy democracies, communities, and our own senses of decency and self-worth. As *The Baffler*'s Jacob Silverman observed, the fact that Facebook "has come to so thoroughly dominate our public sphere is a tragic indictment of American civic life and American techno-capitalism, which has confused the pitiless surveillance of today's internet with utopian empowerment." In other words, we have fucked ourselves royally.

During this decade of Mark Zuckerberg—our very own Kid Z—*Kid A* went from being a dark-hued downer to feel-good entertainment by comparison.

By 2010, *Kid A* was widely considered one of the best albums of the modern era. Even the British music magazines that were initially skeptical came around. In 2006, the *NME* put *Kid A* at number 65 on its list of the greatest British albums *ever,* just ahead of Yorke's boyhood hero Elvis Costello and his pungent expression of revenge and guilt, *This Year's Model.* (Two other Radiohead albums, *The Bends* and *OK Computer,* came in at numbers 11 and 35, respectively.) Also in 2006, *Mojo* put *Kid A* at number 7 on its list of the greatest albums released since 1993. (On that list, *OK Computer* was number 3 and *The Bends* was number 16.)

With any album that is described as *important* or *relevant* or (God help us) *epochal*, the appeal goes beyond just the music. The album must tell us something about ourselves. And the message of *Kid A*, critics decided, related to the Internet. *The Guardian*—which called *Kid A* "a mystifying experience" and "self-consciously awkward and bloody-minded" in two separate pans by different critics in 2000—came around enough on the album to rank it the decade's second-best album, describing it as "a jittery premonition of the troubled, disconnected, overloaded decade to come. The sound of today, in other words, a decade early."

Over at *Rolling Stone*, which put *Kid A* at number 1 on its decade list, the album was credited with "rebuilding rock itself, with a new set of basics and a bleak but potent humanity" that mirrored the online world. And then there was *Pitchfork*, which of course declared *Kid A* the album of the decade while also indulging in some self-mythology. "Nine years ago this month, Brent DiCrescenzo reviewed Radiohead's *Kid A* for this website," wrote the site's managing editor, Mark Richardson. "As far as its rating, no one blinked. Pitchfork was still a blip then, but if you cared at all about the broad sphere of music that included Radiohead, chances are that you heard something very special in *Kid A*. It was that exceptional artifact of modern culture—something about which most people could agree."

The fact that *Kid A* very much was an album that most people could *disagree* about when it was released was easy to set aside in 2010. Nobody was going to cop to not getting a record that had proven to be such a quintessential artifact of the early twenty-first century. The value of *Kid A* as a go-to signifier of How We Live Now couldn't be more thunderously obvious a decade later.

As Richardson put it in his *Pitchfork* blurb, "Radiohead were not only among the first bands to figure out how to use the Internet, but to make their music sound like it."

What's interesting about all of this when I look back at 2010 is that while rock critics had settled on *Kid A* as a warning about how terrible the Internet would become, the Internet actually seems so much better *then* than it does now. It was certainly better if you were a Radiohead fan. Or maybe "freer" is the right word. What right did we have to complain in 2010 anyway? We had no idea how (relatively) good we had it.

For me, 2010 is the year that the Internet started to shrink. I joined Twitter that February, a milestone commemorated by a marker printed in 12-point type and listed below my name and biography on my Twitter landing page. I had resisted joining the site for years before that. My reasons for holding out read like a litany of bad social-media clichés that passed for cutting-edge comedy in the late aughts. ("Who wants to know what I had for breakfast? Isn't that site for losers living in their parents' basement?")

But most of my coworkers where I was employed at the time, *The A.V. Club*, were already enthusiastic users, and they routinely referenced in-jokes, gossip, and kerfuffles that had popped up on the site that day. Also, I kept hearing from fellow music writers about some vital piece of news—mostly related to the big album that week that had inevitably leaked early—they picked up on Twitter. Seemingly overnight, *not* joining Twitter had become a professional liability. So I signed up.

I suspect that the arc of my experience on Twitter is utterly typical. At first, nobody followed me, so I felt compelled to tweet a lot of stupid hot takes because I was (I *am*) a narcissist who needs constant attention. Over time, this strategy kind of worked, and I started getting more likes and retweets, which led to more followers. As my following grew, my tweets became less insane. I learned that making good-natured and self-deprecating jokes about my inherent lameness was a better look on social media than bombastically ranting about how My Morning Jacket's *Circuital* wasn't getting enough respect from the music press.

I had made myself more likeable on social media, in that I was *more self-aware* about the most likeable parts of myself and deliberate about putting them front and center in my tweets. (Like Radiohead, I had heeded the lessons of *The Color of Money* about being myself, but on purpose.) This self-awareness was rewarded with more followers, which meant more likes and retweets, which meant more powerful shots of dopamine bounding through my body.

My coworkers at *The A.V. Club* had always described Twitter as addictive, but I never understood that to be a *literal* description. But Twitter truly was Soma, the recreational drug that provides mindless instant gratification to the populace in Aldous Huxley's dystopian novel *Brave New World*, the *Kid A* of 1932.

Twitter's hold on me was so powerful that it took me years to realize that it had profoundly altered how I used the Internet. I had once started each day with a mental rolodex filled with websites that I wanted to visit. I would cycle through each of them, and typically read an article or two before moving on. But after Twitter, I *only* went to Twitter. I didn't have to go anyplace else. If an article was worth reading, someone in my feed would recommend it. Or else I could just read what they thought about it, and tweet my own joke based on their tweets on an article nobody bothered to actually read beyond the headline.

So that's how my life (and possibly yours) turned out in the future—hooked up to a Soma machine for ten hours a day as the rest of the Internet is increasingly corporatized, consolidated, homogenized, or lobotomized.

But in 2010, the remnants of the older, wilder, and *wider* online world from back when *Kid A* came out hadn't totally fallen away yet. Fan sites like At Ease, Green Plastic, and Follow Me Around were still being updated regularly, and providing space for Radiohead fans to gather and share the latest news and theories about the band.

Each of those sites had originated in the back half of the '90s. One of the oldest fan sites, At Ease, was launched in 1996 by a twenty-three-year-old Dutch man named Adriaan Pels, who had his own at-home Internet connection, a relative luxury at the time. After originally calling his site Pop Is Dead, after the early Radiohead B-side, he renamed it after a lyric in "Fitter Happier."

In time, a moniker that started with "A" played to the advantage of At Ease, as it made the site more likely to stand out on any Radiohead websites that indexed the fan sites. Around the time of *OK Computer*, this corner of the web exploded. In 1997, a twenty-year-old web designer and aspiring photographer named Jonathan Percy started Green Plastic. Follow Me Around also started that year, along with dozens of other sites. When Radiohead overhauled its own website in 1999, ramping up its online presence during the creation of *Kid A* and *Amnesiac*, the band supported the fan communities by linking to them, and even publicly thanked the nascent bloggers for their diligent reporting.

Years before *Wikipedia* or most other online resources, these sites were among the first places where Radiohead fans could go to learn basic information about the band, like a history of their EPs and single releases. It was also a clearinghouse for news items about whatever Radiohead happened to be doing in the studio or on the road. Again, at a time when people relied on magazines and MTV for the latest music news, a site like At Ease was a daily pit stop for many Radiohead fans as more and more of them migrated online.

But then people stopped visiting sites outside the social-media platforms. Even if you still loved Radiohead, you loved your feeds on Twitter, Facebook, or Instagram more. Not long after the ten-year anniversary of *Kid A* came and went, many of the old fan sites that started in the late '90s slowly turned into graveyards. The people who ran them started to drift away. They were no longer in their twenties. They were adults with jobs and families and interests beyond arguing whether *The Bends* was better than *OK Computer*.

But many of us didn't *need* to go to fan sites anymore. You could just . . . stay on Twitter or Reddit or some other social-media platform. One must always keep the Soma machine plugged in.

Social media transformed the web into a hall of mirrors in which your own opinions and preferences are distorted and re-flected back at you, to the point where any other reality is pitched outside the frame and therefore rendered nonexistent, as long as you have curated your feed correctly. It is like living inside your own head for every hour of the day, only the voices ringing around in your skull don't always belong to you. Though they always kind of *sound* like you, which is good enough.

For all of the talk about *Kid A* mimicking the disjointed language and claustrophobia of the Internet, the web didn't feel like *that* when the album was released, nor did it really feel that way ten years after the fact. While the aughts were a time of massive trauma in nearly all areas of public life—caused by war, terrorism, duplicitous governments, and a mass-media system that was breaking down and drifting toward an à la carte "choose your own reality" pluralism—it still felt like the Internet was a place where truth, intelligence, and individuality might still reign.

But as the second decade of the twenty-first century commenced, the Internet felt less and less like a place where weirdos and outsiders could escape. It's where you yearned to escape *from*. On Twitter, there's a long tradition of users making grandiose announcements about officially leaving social media, and cleansing themselves of the pernicious influence that it has on their lives. And then, inevitably, those people always come back. They can't help themselves.

I know because I've been there. I've deleted the Twitter app on my phone about ten thousand times. I've tried to set guidelines about never posting on the weekend, or refraining from scrolling when I'm supposed to be reading bedtime stories to my kids. I always fail.

Everybody wants to be a friend and nobody wants to be a slave. But in the end, I'm Twitter's bitch.

CHAPTER 10

TRUE LOVE WAITS

They made their intentions known years in advance. If inducted into the Rock & Roll Hall of Fame, Radiohead did not plan to show up.

"I don't care," Jonny Greenwood said flatly in a 2017 *Rolling Stone* interview. Thom Yorke wasn't any more enthusiastic. "Don't ask me things like that. I always put my foot in my mouth."

Perhaps as a form of punishment for their insolence, the Rock Hall didn't actually induct Radiohead in 2018, the first year they were eligible. Of course, nearly all of the most crucial influences on *Kid A*—Can, Kraftwerk, Fela Kuti, Eno—weren't in yet either. Getting rejected by this institution almost seemed like a sign of respect, especially given that Bon Jovi and the Moody Blues made it that year instead of Radiohead.

In 2019, however, it finally happened. And while Thom, Jonny, and Colin—who actually said he'd feel "grateful" to be inducted in that *Rolling Stone* interview—declined to attend, it came as no surprise that the two members who did show up were Ed O'Brien and Phil Selway. The rock-history guy and the rock-steady guy.

David Byrne inducted them. *Remain in Light* was a blueprint for *Kid A*, and the trajectory of both revolutionary albums had brought the head Talking Head and two-fifths of Radiohead to the Barclays Center in Brooklyn for a ceremony honoring the world's most dubious musical museum.

Byrne's speech was charmingly low-key and tossed-off. "I was surprised and very flattered when Radiohead stated they named themselves after a song that I had written," he said with a boyish sincerity belying that his sixty-seventh birthday was just a month and a half away.

The song in question was culled from the soundtrack of Byrne's first and only feature film as a director, 1986's *True Stories*. "Radiohead" was not one of the band's greatest hits. It wasn't even a treasured deep cut. "I did ask myself, 'Why that song?' I still haven't been able to figure it out, and in a certain way I don't want to know," Byrne said quizzically. "This was kind of a goofy Tex-Mex song that I'd written. Maybe we'll find out, who knows."

After a short video tribute, Phil and Ed entered the stage. "I'd just like to say a little bit about what being in Radiohead means to me," Phil began, reading nervously from index cards. This was his debut as an unlikely arena-rock frontman. "It can be awkward and challenging sometimes. But I guess that's what kept us all interested for the past three decades. I'm beyond proud of what the five of us have achieved together, and I know that Radiohead wouldn't have become what it is without the five of us."

Ed similarly focused his brief comments on the sanctity of the band members' bond. He spoke touchingly about the "transcendental moments" that can occur when the five of them are in the studio or onstage together. And he expressed gratitude for their friendship.

"We could've done this without this love for one another but there's such a deep, deep bond and it's a beautiful thing," he concluded. "So thank you. I love you."

Radiohead's Rock Hall induction was, in its own weird way, perfectly appropriate. They had always managed to have it both ways. They were both the ultimate outsiders, *and* a highly profitable and esteemed mainstream rock band. With *Kid A*, they made their most controversial record *and* achieved their first number-one album in the United States. Now at the Rock Hall, they managed to both shrug rebelliously *and* express genuine appreciation for the honor.

Coming in the midst of their fourth decade as a band, the Rock Hall induction also served as a benchmark in Radiohead's evolution into a full-blown classic-rock act, a fact that the band members—at least Thom and Jonny—have never fully accepted *while also* not completely rejecting it out of hand.

Since the start of the twenty-first century, they had strenuously positioned themselves outside of that old-school rock continuum. In his speech, Byrne praised Radiohead as much for how they challenged the music business as he did for their actual music. The online outreach of *Kid A* and the "pay what you want" dynamic of *In Rainbows* were attempts to circumvent the bad old record industry, in order to foster a more direct and virtuous band-audience relationship. It was, at heart, about reimagining the very nature of rock stardom.

But rock stardom was already in the process of being taken apart by a record industry now preoccupied with pop and hip-hop. What was left two decades after *Kid A*, ironically, was the stature and status of Radiohead, one of the last legacy bands left standing that still had some traces of relevance for emerging generations.

The significance of Phil and Ed dwelling at the Rock Hall induction on the relationship between the five original guys couldn't have been lost on the institution's membership, many of whom were part of bands that had long since been trans-formed into *brands* with only one or two flagship members. In the 2010s, Radiohead's grandest achievement wasn't artistic or even business-related. It was merely their insistence on not falling apart, and choosing instead to reinvest themselves in their own history and foundational strengths.

Here's an analogy that amateur rock historian Ed O'Brien might appreciate (while also finding it slightly dispiriting): Radio-head at the time of the Rock Hall induction had reached its *Steel Wheels* period. I refer to the 1989 Rolling Stones record that sig-naled their comeback after a fallow period in the mid-'80s, when the band nearly broke up amid very public acrimony between Mick Jagger and Keith Richards over their respective solo careers.

In the '10s, the members of Radiohead were just as wrapped up in their own side projects as the Stones had been in the '80s, though they thankfully kept their dirty laundry out of the public eye. But whenever they came back, their power derived from *still* being here.

The Stones were the rare band to not only survive the '60s but thrive during the subsequent decades. By the time I saw them at age sixteen on the *Voodoo Lounge* tour in 1994, they *were* the

'60s. For kids like me who were obsessed with the era but only knew it from a distance, the Stones were our shiniest and most vital link to that long-lost world.

Radiohead similarly outlived nearly every other Generation X cliché in order to headline Coachella in the distant future known as 2017. The children of '90s Radiohead fans wanted to see them for the same reason that I had wanted to see Mick and Keith play "Satisfaction" as a teenager. Radiohead was a national landmark now, a musical mope-rock Mount Rushmore, a symbol of rock's stubborn refusal to disappear completely.

If you manage to stick around long enough as a rock band, you will inevitably begin to repeat yourself, even when you go out of your way to not repeat yourself.

For Radiohead, the process of making their eighth album, 2011's *The King of Limbs*, echoed the creation of *Kid A* one decade prior. Just as Thom Yorke had contemplated a dramatic shake-up in how the band would function in 1999, he publicly speculated in 2009 about whether Radiohead would even continue to make albums.

"None of us want to go into that creative hoo-ha of a long-play record again," he mused to *The Believer*. He was still burned out from the years-long deliberations over *In Rainbows*. "I mean, it's just become a real drag. It worked with *In Rainbows* because we had a real fixed idea about where we were going. But we've all said that we can't possibly dive into that again. It'll kill us."

But even as Yorke complained publicly that he didn't want the "hoo-ha" of making a new Radiohead album, a new Radiohead album was already secretly under way. Though the band had once again decided to reevaluate their own haphazard creative process. Reflecting on *The King of Limbs* in 2012, Jonny Greenwood said they "didn't want to pick up guitars and write chord sequences. We didn't want to sit in front of a computer either. We wanted a third thing, which involved playing and programming."

The album unfolded as *The Eraser* had, with the band recording drum, bass, and guitar parts, which were then sampled, looped, thoroughly fucked with, and then reassembled into songs. Thom and Jonny were in the driver's seat, with the former handling melodies and lyrics and the latter overseeing the software program used to sample the instruments.

The result was a record that had all of the components of a Radiohead release, but without the feel or the energy of an actual band. On paper, it represented another progression beyond the usual conventions for guitar-based music. It also carried forward the innovations of *Kid A*, which essentially had been a rock band emulating the sound and methodology of electronic artists. With *The King of Limbs*, Radiohead located a genuine DMZ between rock and DJ-oriented music. The album didn't really belong in either category, but rather in its own world. Radiohead had proven they no longer had to ape the style of others. They could reinvent themselves *by* themselves.

But as music, and not just as an artistic gesture, *The King of Limbs* was easy to admire and difficult to love. For all of the album's ingenuity, it also seemed kind of slight. While Radiohead was as adventurous as ever, experimenting at every turn, the songs didn't feel all that powerful emotionally. There were some minor exceptions, and they tended to be the most direct and least fussed-over tracks, like the piano ballad "Codex" and the wistful album-closer "Separator," in which Yorke sings, "If you think this is over / then you're wrong." The lyric prompted some fans to speculate (wrongly) about whether the thirty-seven-minute *Limbs*, by far the shortest Radiohead album, was actually the first half of a two-part LP.

The nagging feeling of insignificance that hounded *The King of Limbs* upon its release in 2011 was compounded by *how* it was released. As was the case with *In Rainbows*, they announced the album one week in advance, and then they dropped a download online, with a compact-disc release following one month later.

The media had changed a lot since 2007, when *In Rainbows* had managed to stay in the conversation for weeks after its release. Whereas *Kid A* had been among the first major rock albums to be heard and discussed online, *The King of Limbs* was one of the first major "event" records I remember tracking primarily via social media. Instead of reading and debating album reviews produced by major music publications, fans now were more likely to talk about the album on Twitter, "live-tweeting" each track as they heard it for the first time. Some random lunatic could now tweet "Morning Mr. Magpie . . . more like Mr. Shitpie" two seconds after hearing the record and potentially reach as many readers as a professional critic who carefully crafted a two-thousand-word thinkpiece. This fundamentally changed (and probably destroyed) professional music writing as we know it.

And then . . . the album swiftly disappeared. There were, after all, new albums to live-tweet. *The King of Limbs* was just another piece of pop-cultural data that was consumed, digested, and flushed away in the span of twenty-four or so hours. None of this was lost on Radiohead. "It was amazing to just put the record out like that," Yorke told *Rolling Stone* in 2012. "But then it didn't feel like it really existed."

It didn't help that Radiohead played only three shows in 2011, opting instead to mount a proper tour in support of *The King of Limbs* the following year. I saw Radiohead that summer at a miserable shed outside of Chicago. Incredibly, it was my first time seeing Radiohead. In the mid-'90s, Radiohead played every two-bit music venue in America four or five times, and yet I never made a point to see one of the great rock bands of my lifetime play some of my favorite songs of the era. It wasn't until their tours became infrequent, and they were touring in support of an album I didn't particularly like, that I drove more than two hours to sit in an uncomfortable folding chair with twenty-four thousand fellow Radiohead fans.

It wasn't a great show. My favorite memory is when they played "Everything in Its Right Place" at the end of the first encore. It was electrifying to hear the crowd light up like a pack of Lynyrd Skynyrd fanatics hearing the opening chords of "Free Bird," given how flat and uninvolving the rest of the show was.

I've since come around on *The King of Limbs* as an album and tour, thanks to some excellent bootlegs that permitted me to actually hear how Radiohead transformed those songs live, without having to suffer through terrible outdoor amphitheater acoustics. Radiohead had uncovered a lot of the power of the *Kid A* and *Amnesiac* songs on the road, and for *The King of Limbs* embracing their vitality as a band had yet again served them well. Though they had also grown beyond the core five, with second drummer Clive Deamer offering vital assistance by helping them to open up the songs rhythmically.

"Didn't they say when the Beatles got Billy Preston everybody was on best behavior?" Ed O'Brien observed in *Rolling Stone*, coming up (of course) with a pertinent analogy to another legacy rock band. "Having someone break up the energy—that's good. It got people out of old habits."

Six days after I saw Radiohead on the *King of Limbs* North American tour, the band arrived in Toronto for the campaign's final concert. During the setup that afternoon, the roof of the temporary stage collapsed. Three members of the crew were injured, and drum technician Scott Johnson was killed instantly. Radiohead managed to pull it together after the tragedy to perform the European dates, but once the tour ended later that year the band entered another long hiatus.

Thom Yorke formed a new band, Atoms for Peace, with Flea from the Red Hot Chili Peppers. By then, he had adopted Los Angeles as a home. He described the making of AFP's 2013 album, *Amok*, thusly: "We were at Flea's house. We got wasted, played pool and listened to Fela Kuti all night."

It sounds a lot more fun than the making of any Radiohead album, though the end product was also less noteworthy than any Radiohead album. *Amok* has its share of pleasures; I'm partial to "Default," a sexy dancing death-bot synth ballad that would have seriously livened up *The King of Limbs*. But the album overall felt like a reiteration of Yorke's fascination with using skilled rock musicians to create component music parts that he could later piece together on his computer. It repeated what *The King of Limbs* had borrowed from *The Eraser*, and what *The Eraser* had underlined from *Kid A*.

Also disconcerting during this period was the Californication of Thom Yorke's personal style. The man who was always preternaturally suspicious of rock stars was now looking more and more like a caricature of an aging rock dude. This description from a 2017 *Rolling Stone* profile was especially alarming: "At the moment, he's sitting in Little Dom's Italian restaurant in the Los Feliz neighborhood of his adopted hometown of Los Angeles, wearing a bleached denim jacket with the collar popped up, a thin white T-shirt and what appear to be leather pants. His long hair is pulled back into a tiny, tight bun; he has a stylish gray beard."

Yorke's graying man bun was an apt metaphor for the state of Radiohead's music. One of rock's most uncomfortable bands—to the point where they actually fetishized their discomfort as an essential part of the creative process—was finally taking it easy. They were rich, successful, and enjoying the spoils of their elevated status. In 1992, Thom Yorke had taken a cheeky shot at Jim Morrison. Now he was wearing Jim Morrison's leather pants.

I don't point this out with any malice. From Yorke's perspective, I can imagine that *Amok* or his 2014 solo record, *Tomorrow's Modern Boxes*—released as a paid-for BitTorrent bundle, officially the most gimmicky and tiresome Radiohead-related release strategy—were freeing precisely because they *weren't* considered so damn important. Sometimes, you just want to make a record. And you'd love it if people would just take it for what it is. That, in a way, is what Yorke wanted all along for *Kid A*, an album without any overt lyrical meaning. Only now he was in the part of his career when the world was willing to give him more space and less attention.

After they've delivered so many of the most monumental albums of my lifetime, I firmly believe that Radiohead had earned the right to not be so hard on themselves. You don't have to make *Kid A* in your fifties. Your fifties are about discovering that there's more to life than making an album like *Kid A*.

Besides, life in middle age can already be painful enough. As litigation from the Toronto stage collapse lingered, Yorke also grappled with the separation from his longtime partner, Rachel Owen, in 2015. The following year, in December of 2016, she died of cancer at the age of forty-eight.

The breakup and preemptive feeling of loss were widely presumed to have influenced Radiohead's downcast and hopelessly pretty ninth LP, *A Moon Shaped Pool*, which came out in May of 2016. Though the album was hardly a song cycle composed in a finite amount of time. It was—to make another Rolling Stones analogy—their *Tattoo You*, a patchwork of older material fashioned to sound like a cohesive, resonant whole. The fiery opening track, "Burn the Witch," originated all the way back in the *Kid A/ Amnesiac* period. "Present Tense" had been performed by Yorke at a solo concert in 2009, and two other numbers, "Identikit" and "Ful Stop," had been performed during the *King of Limbs* tour.

The song that made fans swoon the most was also of the oldest vintage. "True Love Waits" had been a well-known part of Radiohead's mythology since the mid-'90s, buoyed by a devastating bootleg recording of the song's debut on December 5, 1995, during a concert at the Luna Theatre in Brussels. A plaintive ballad, "True Love Waits" can be read both as an extremely earnest love song, and a comment on extremely earnest love songs— when Yorke sings "I'll drown my beliefs / to have your babies," you detect an arched eyebrow, but it's not *that* arched. It's another instance of Radiohead managing to have it both ways, though they ultimately err on the side of crushing vulnerability.

They tried to record it for *OK Computer*, and then during the *Kid A/Amnesiac* era. In his journal, Ed O'Brien mentioned "True Love Waits" as a song that had "been kicking around for about four years now and each time we approached it we seemed to be going down the same old paths. It actually sounds like the start of something exciting now." The band actually played the song in Tel Aviv on July 8, 2000—the first time "True Love Waits" appeared in a Radiohead setlist since the Brussels gig. But no matter Ed's apparent enthusiasm, the song still didn't make either album.

In 2001, "True Love Waits" finally appeared on an official Radiohead LP, the live EP *I Might Be Wrong*. It's a ragged, delicate Yorke solo acoustic performance recorded in Oslo that doesn't have the distinctive prog-rock keyboard percolations from the Brussels version. It nonetheless became a go-to closing track for countless mixtapes—for the true believers who kept actual cassette tapes alive in the early aughts—though Nigel Godrich later referred to it as a "shitty version" of the song.

"True Love Waits" continued to appear in live setlists for tours in support of *In Rainbows* and *The King of Limbs*. When Yorke played it in his solo shows, he always referred to it as a lost song that Radiohead had never been able to master. This is how it is with this band—most Radiohead fans would agree that they did a perfect "True Love Waits," way back in Brussels, the first time they ever played it live. But that was also the simplest, most direct, most *obvious* version. Radiohead couldn't let themselves be satisfied with it.

Finally, on *A Moon Shaped Pool*, they felt like they cracked it. Gone was the acoustic guitar and the *Close to the Edge* synth. What was left was Yorke's despondent, resplendent vocal, set against ethereal piano tinkling that sounded like Thelonious Monk trying to play like Philip Glass. In the process, "True Love Waits" changed from a half-serious/half-cheeky lament of a lovesick young man to a eulogy performed by a middle-aged father who had arrived at a deeper understanding of love's power and limitations.

This wasn't the story of just one song, but also of a band. If you knew nothing about Radiohead's career other than the story of "True Love Waits," from that bootleg recording captured in Belgium to the song's eventual appearance twenty-one years later on A *Moon Shaped Pool*, you would still know everything crucial about their life as a band.

It was ultimately a more challenging path to the same heartfelt destination. Impossible, tedious, and potentially self-destructive. The only path for Radiohead.

Because he's now a rock star in his fifties who occasionally wears leather pants and dons a man bun, Thom Yorke has to face the usual questions about whether Radiohead is a nostalgia act.

If you're in a band that has spanned multiple decades, and even multiple centuries, you will have accumulated a past that stretches as far back as the future once seemed when you were young. Which is why, as you get older, you start to care less about where you're going. Instead, you're more interested in figuring out how you got where you are. You realize there are parts of yourself that you no longer recognize, or even remember once existed. The past is at once familiar and weirdly *unfamiliar*. If you delve deep enough, you might find that you don't really know who you ever really *were*. You'll also discover the ways in which you've never changed, even from the time you were a child, your very own Kid A.

Many of us go to therapy in order to turn over the rocks in our subconscious that our past selves live under. But when you're in a rock band, you see the person you used to be everywhere—on old album covers, in ancient music videos, in setlists of songs you wrote several lifetimes ago. Being a successful musician means playacting all of your past traumas, and retaining your old identities like a collection of ratty sock puppets.

"I'm also fascinated to look back on what we've done, and try and remember who the hell it was who wrote that, or who the hell it was who played it," Yorke said in a 2019 radio interview. "Because oftentimes, we're halfway through the song, and I'm asking myself, 'How on earth did we get to this point? How did we find this?' Because I don't remember it—I'm looking at it from so far away. I don't remember the process. I guess I'm still working and doing new things all the time, we all are, so it doesn't really bother me. If we were touring endlessly, playing the same stuff, then you'd be talking to a different person right now."

Yorke at the time was promoting his fourth solo album, *Anima*, which included the very best Radiohead (or Radiohead-adjacent) music of the 2010s. The album's highlight is "Dawn Chorus," in which Yorke sings about dread, reinvention, and death over a rudimentary, digitally warped keyboard lick. "If you could do it all again / yeah, without a second thought," he sings. "I think I missed something / but I'm not sure what."

It's the sound of a man looking back to the person he was twenty years earlier—when he was lost and depressed and embittered but committed to reinventing himself and his band, even at the risk of his own sanity. Thom Yorke is still that person he was during the *Kid A* era, but also not. They are connected but strangers. That person got him to where he is, but now he's gone, forever. Only the music remains as a link between these different versions of himself . . . and it also links us to him.

Anima will never have the stature of *Kid A*, an album that sought to discover the future and put it inside the ears of a generation just entering a scary, fractured, and deeply troubled new century. Nobody looks to Radiohead now to make the masterpiece that will define our present moment. Thom Yorke is no longer the sort of artist who can seek out what's ahead of us. There are newer, younger artists for that, as there should be. Yorke's role now is to explore his own past, to dialogue with it, to reconnect with what was lost and how we were changed by what we gained. You can call that nostalgia. But it's more akin to excavation, uncovering long-lost worlds so that we might once again be connected to that which we can no longer see or touch, and yet still *feel* is elemental.

That's what I hear now when I listen to *Kid A*—a desperation to not feel disconnected from one another, our environment, our very own souls or whatever the essence of who we are is. Radiohead diagnosed this malaise at the heart of so many of us at the dawn of the twenty-first century. And then they (perhaps unwittingly) offered themselves up as a remedy, creating music that has provided a common thread in our own personal narratives, a rare constant presence amid so much change and disruption. Even as everything else in your life has been turned over since the first time you heard "Creep," you still have your relationship with this band's music. Even when Radiohead themselves have felt lost, they've provided ballast to so many of us for decades.

You can hear the common anxieties that bonded so many of us back then in *Kid A*—about technology, about globalism, about the precarious state of truth and decency in our political lives. Radiohead conveyed these chaotic feelings with free-jazz horn sections and Aphex Twin–inspired glitches and other musical flourishes that might seem corny or outdated now. But the vibe of this record—the uncertainty, the darkness, the abject fear that things will only grow worse—has felt like a constant in our world ever since.

This umbilical cord of dread that connects us to *Kid A* is oddly reassuring. And I don't think this is related *just* to nostalgia. After all, nostalgia has a way of embalming the past, sucking out what was once vital and messy and flushing it out with nothingness, so that it resembles what it was but is, at heart, hollow and lifeless. It's like that scene in Thomas Pynchon's *Inherent Vice*, with the hippie detective Doc Sportello and his lawyer, Sauncho Smilax, spying in the distance the mythical schooner *Golden Fang* after it has been fully cleansed, literally and metaphorically, of its "dark residues of blood and betrayal." *Kid A*, mercifully, is not that.

When I think about the world that *Kid A* evokes, I don't feel envy for the past, as a nostalgist does. I think about rigged elections, terrorist attacks, phony wars, and the Internet devolving into a misinformation network. I think about the decline of rock music and how once-diverse platforms for music distribution and conversation have been homogenized. And I marvel at how *Kid A* seemed to soundtrack all of these changes.

I also feel a rush of gratitude that we survived it all. Which means we might just yet survive whatever apocalypse looms on our present horizon. *Kid A* is no longer an album about how scary the future is. It is now an album about how scary the past was, and how we found a way to make it to where we are now.

Yesterday I woke up sucking a lemon. With any luck, I will wake up sucking a lemon tomorrow too.

ACKNOWLEDGMENTS

Thanks as always to my agent, Anthony Mattero, and this time to my editor, Ben Schafer. Jeff Blehar was a technical adviser and the supplier of many incredible Radiohead bootlegs. Charlotte Goddu made sure everything was factually correct.

I am indebted to the *Citizen Insane* blog, which was an invaluable resource when I couldn't get my hands on primary sources. I also relied upon the work of these writers and critics: Mac Randall, Marvin Lin, Chuck Klosterman, Nick Kent, Simon Reynolds, Brent DiCrescenzo, Jon Pareles, Alex Ross, and Jeremy Gordon.

Thanks to Radiohead for making this music.

Nothing would be in its right place without Val, Hen, and Ro.

INDEX